AF228379

LEFT FOR DEAD AT NIJMEGEN

LEFT FOR DEAD AT NIJMEGEN

The True Story of an American Paratrooper in WWII

MARCUS A. NANNINI

CASEMATE

Philadelphia & Oxford

Published in the United States of America and Great Britain in 2019 by
CASEMATE PUBLISHERS
1950 Lawrence Road, Havertown, PA 19083, USA
and
The Old Music Hall, 106–108 Cowley Road, Oxford OX4 1JE, UK

Copyright © 2019 Marcus A. Nannini

Hardback Edition: ISBN 978-1-61200-696-3
Digital Edition: ISBN 978-1-61200-697-0 (ePub)

A CIP record for this book is available from the British Library

Printed and bound in the United States of America

Typeset in India by Versatile PreMedia Services. www.versatilepremedia.com

For a complete list of Casemate titles, please contact:

CASEMATE PUBLISHERS (US)
Telephone (610) 853-9131
Fax (610) 853-9146
Email: casemate@casematepublishers.com
www.casematepublishers.com

CASEMATE PUBLISHERS (UK)
Telephone (01865) 241249
Email: casemate-uk@casematepublishers.co.uk
www.casematepublishers.co.uk

Front cover: Sketch of German soldier by Gene Metcalfe

"I speak in the name of the entire German people when I assure the world that we all share the honest wish to eliminate the enmity that brings far more costs than any possible benefits.
It would be a wonderful thing for all of humanity if both peoples would renounce force against each other forever.
The German people are ready to make such a pledge."

Adolf Hitler, Chancellor of Germany, October 14, 1933

Contents

Prologue

As you read the following true story you may feel fear, anguish, sorrow, pain, shock, and maybe even dread.

The subject of the story certainly felt those emotions but considered himself to be taking part in a grand adventure on a scale he never imagined while growing up in rural America during the 1930s and early 1940s.

A teenager when he entered service to his country, and not older than 22 when he came home, he had no time to grow up, for he found himself thrust into the depths of a war, the likes of which the world had never witnessed. He rose to his respective challenges without complaint and performed above and beyond what most people today might consider a reasonable expectation.

As Gene Metcalfe boarded a C-47 paratroop transport plane to fly him to a drop zone outside of Nijmegen, Holland, in the first wave of Operation *Market Garden*, an upbeat British lieutenant handed him an unmarked cardboard box containing 12 dozen condoms. A mere 12 hours later Gene considered them to have been a bad joke as he found himself being interrogated by Heinrich Himmler deep in the bowels of a Charlemagne-era castle, machine gun-toting fanatics of the Reichsführer "SS" on either side of him.

The following are his recollections as explained to Marcus A. Nannini in a series of interviews conducted over the course of several years. The conversations, characters, and scenes set forth in this story are recreated to the best of Gene's memory. The presence of Heinrich Himmler on the night of September 17/18, 1944, has not proven capable of independent verification. The search for definitive proof of his whereabouts on the night in question continues.

During the course of more than two dozen interviews, Gene was consistent in his recollections and especially with details, down to counting the number of stairs in Belvedere Castle at Nijmegen. Some of the conversations with his German captors are Gene's interpretation of the original dialogues, most of which were part sign language, part German and part English. He occasionally uses incorrect German words as he pronounces the German language as he heard it in 1944/45, not necessarily as it was actually pronounced. His hearing was significantly compromised as a result of his right eardrum having been irreparably destroyed by a German "88" while at the same time losing some hearing in his left ear.

A special thank-you to First Lieutenant/Flight Instructor, veteran of 27 combat missions, recipient of three air medals, seven battle stars and Market Garden veteran, Harry E. Watson, USAAF (Retired) and Major Robert Bauman, USAF (Retired).

Thank you to my editor, Susanne C. Johnson, M.A.

CHAPTER ONE

Homework

It was a cold, dreary Tuesday morning, November 10, 1942. Nineteen-year-old Gene Metcalfe was attending his much dreaded math class at DeKalb High School in the small teachers college and farming town of DeKalb, Illinois. The class had finally settled down after dutifully handing in their respective homework assignments to their teacher, Mr. Hoppe.

Gene was not-so-patiently waiting for Hoppe to discover his homework was missing. He fidgeted in his seat as Hoppe slowly worked his way through the assignments. He watched Hoppe carefully marking off the names from the class list as he slowly progressed to the bottom of the stack of homework papers. Finally, after what seemed for Gene to have taken far too long, Hoppe, with a flamboyant flip of his fingers, dropped his pencil and looked directly at him.

"Mr. Metcalfe?" There was only the slightest hint of interest in his voice, which was just a notch above his usual monotone. Gene, being respectful, stood in response.

"Yes Sir?" It took all of his willpower to keep from laughing.

"Didn't you do your homework last night, Mr. Metcalfe?" Hoppe's tone of voice revealed his annoyance, which provided Gene with a little satisfaction for all the times he had struggled in Hoppe's class over the last two and a half years.

"No Sir, I did not. In fact, I don't plan to ever do math homework again." Gene no longer could hide a smile, aggravating Hoppe all the more. Hoppe stood in response to the unexpected answer while simultaneously raising the level of his voice.

"Mr. Metcalfe!" He paused to assure himself he commanded everyone's attention. "Just how do *you* expect to graduate next June if you don't do your homework?"

"Sir," he replied, "I don't expect to graduate. In fact, I've just joined the 508th Paratroop Infantry Regiment and I'm leaving right this minute to report for duty!" He began to move toward the doorway and paused to deliver one final thought: "In a few months they're going to have me parachuting right down on top of Hitler's head when he's at that mountaintop retreat of his so we can end the war!"

Without hesitating, Gene quickly walked up the aisle, right past an uncharacteristically quiet Mr. Hoppe and out the classroom door. Hoppe remained standing, his mouth wide open and a look of complete surprise on his face as Gene made his escape, the door quietly closing behind him.

It was obvious to the entire class Gene's response was the last thing Hoppe expected to hear. In fact, they were all shocked, for he hadn't spoken of his enlistment with any of his friends. A fellow senior, Betty, didn't want to believe what she had just witnessed. She was confused, furious, and devastated. She hesitated a few moments, and before Hoppe could regain his composure she bolted out the door and down the hallway in pursuit of Gene.

She caught up with him just as he was pushing open the heavy wooden door he'd sooner never pass through again, frantically calling out his name. Gene considered for a moment whether he should wait and decided he owed her at least some explanation.

He turned to look at her for what he considered to be the last time. Betty's haystack-colored hair was pulled back into a long ponytail. Her blue eyes were the unspoiled accent to her perfectly oval-shaped face, her nose turning up ever so slightly above what had become a set of quivering, red-lipsticked lips. Those quivering lips had been Gene's weak spot since early in their relationship but now he was duty-bound to the Army. Quivering lips or not, he wasn't going to be caving in to her desires.

With tears streaming down her cheeks, she expressed some understanding of his need to join the war effort. She told him she was under the impression they had agreed he would wait to enlist until after graduation so they could get married. She wanted to know what had happened to their plans to go to the local teachers college, graduate, get teaching jobs, have children, and spend their lives together.

As gently as Gene knew how, he explained the plans she spoke of were her plans and he had never agreed to them. He felt it would be better if he volunteered now and let fate dictate what happens to them. Her tears continued to flow as they embraced and shared a final brief and gentle kiss. Gene turned and quickly slipped through the heavy door. Betty blocked it from slamming shut with her foot. She stuck her head through the door and, sounding more hopeful than certain, she called out to him: "Gene, I'll write you!"

Gene turned his head and paused just long enough to say: "That'd be swell, if you want to."

Gene was due to report for duty at Camp Grant in Rockford, Illinois, the following morning and was focused on getting himself there on time. Rockford was about 40 miles away from his old clapboard home in DeKalb. Given it was mid-November, the distance was too far for him to cover on foot and he knew his folks wouldn't help either. Though they had adopted him as an infant, his experiences told him his parents were not particularly supportive of any of his efforts.

He was a sports star at DeKalb High School, having lettered in basketball, but his parents never revealed much interest in his high school efforts, let alone attend even one of his events. Now and again he would share with his pal Jimmy the fact his mother on numerous occasions had make it painfully clear to him: "Although you are my only child, you are not necessarily my favorite." In fact, when he was about eight years old one of his mom's friends lost her only child, a boy, in a freak accident. At his own mother's suggestion she sent Gene to live with the woman and her husband for an entire year, allegedly to help them overcome their grief. He barely ever saw either of his adopted parents during his year away.

In addition to being a naturally gifted athlete, Gene was an accomplished piano player. But no matter how hard he tried, and he gave it his best, he never could seem to elicit very much in the way of loving emotions from his mom. Her fondness for the piano had motivated him to learn the instrument in the first place. Unfortunately, his piano playing never appeared to have much in the way of an emotive effect on her. Still, he had a love for music and thoroughly enjoyed playing at home and at the homes of his many friends.

Art was another of his talents. A naturally gifted artist, he possessed the unique ability to beautifully recreate any scene, or person, from memory. If he noticed an interesting individual or location, he could recreate it on canvas many months later as if the subject were still directly in front of him.

He shrugged off the disinterest of his parents and applied himself to sports, the arts, and school, except for math, a class he believed to be the epitome of boredom. He considered himself to be pretty much on his own in life and seldom looked outside of himself for help.

About a year earlier he had been on a double-date at the local theater where the exciting Edmond O'Brien movie, *Parachute Battalion*, was the main feature. From that point forward he decided he would become a paratrooper, even though America had not yet been drawn into the war. He appreciated the fact paratroopers packed their own 'chutes and were responsible to themselves.

He had missed an entire year of school with a severe illness when he was very young, making him a year older than most of his classmates. He originally decided he would stay in school until he graduated but found it impossible to wait any longer and enlisted in the paratroopers on the afternoon of November 9, 1942. He would be reporting for duty on Armistice Day, November 11. However, his first order of business consisted of finding a way to get himself to Rockford as quickly as possible.

With only one primary road leading to Rockford, Gene began hitchhiking as soon as he reached the two-lane highway stretching out across miles and miles of harvested corn fields. He'd been trying to hitch a ride for nearly an hour when a black, two-door Ford businessman's coupe pulled over. As he ran up to the car the driver pushed open the passenger door. Gene noticed a cloud of cigarette smoke pour out of the little coupe. He didn't smoke and rationalized to himself: "A ride's a ride."

He hopped into the front seat, thanked the driver, and introduced himself. The driver offered him a cigarette and stated his name was "Johnson, just Johnson."

"So where ya head'n Gene?" Johnson asked.

"Rockford, Sir. I've joined the paratroopers and need to report for duty at Camp Grant first thing tomorrow morning."

Gene recalls Johnson said to him that was "downright fine." He told Gene he felt the paratroopers sure must be brave jumping out of perfectly good aircraft like they do. Johnson also told him: "I admire your courage."

Johnson went on to explain there was no way you'd find him jumping out of a plane or even find him in a plane. He told Gene: "It ain't natural."

Johnson snuffed out the butt of his cigarette and immediately lit another; Gene soon discovered he was a chain-smoker. As he was about to return the cigarettes to his shirt pocket, he stopped and offered the pack to Gene.

"No thanks, Sir, I don't smoke," Gene responded.

"Take my word, kid, you're better if ya don't take up the habit; it may damn well kill you someday."

After about 20 minutes of silence Johnson slightly let up on the gas pedal and asked Gene if he knew where he was going to spend the night, especially since it was below freezing. Gene had been pondering exactly the same question and explained he'd never given it much thought until then. He said his only concern was to be on time for reporting to Camp Grant in the morning.

Johnson drove a few more minutes when Gene noticed he was smiling. He told Gene he had an answer to his problem. Before explaining himself, he paused to light another cigarette. After taking a couple of puffs he proceeded to say he was buddies with just about everybody on the Rockford police force and was "damn near-certain" they'd be honored to put Gene up for the night. He said they'd probably feed him too.

Gene considered the offer for a few moments and responded: "Well, so long as they don't lock me in a cell, that'd be just swell. Thanks!"

Gene relaxed and gazed out at the nearly barren farm fields, his mind wandering to the days he had hunted pheasants and rabbits in similar fields as the annual season opened in November each year. This November, however, there'd be no small game hunting, as he had only one thing in mind: joining the 508th Parachute Infantry Regiment.

Johnson proceeded to drive Gene to the Rockford police station. After thanking Johnson, Gene introduced himself to the desk sergeant;

a balding, older man Gene thought looked like a grandfather he never had. He immediately took a liking to him and told the sergeant he was reporting to the 508th Paratroop Infantry Regiment the following morning and needed a place to sleep.

The sergeant greeted him with a hero's reception. After vigorously shaking Gene's hand, he directed one of his officers to triple up the mattresses in their "best cell." When Gene thanked him, he addressed the sergeant by his rank. The sergeant immediately replied: "Just call me Frank. You'll have your own sergeant soon enough!" Frank went on to say the Rockford Police Department would be "right proud" to put him up for the night. He told Gene they'd also feed him and drive him to Camp Grant in the morning. Gene was hugely relieved as the alternative would have meant sleeping on a sidewalk.

Frank motioned toward a pair of officers sitting nearby and ordered them to lend him a hand setting up cell eight. The two men jumped to their feet and were immediately on Gene's heels as the group proceeded through a doorway and deeper into the building.

Upon arriving at cell eight, Frank directed the pair of officers to carry in a padded armchair. Frank, a quizzical expression on his face, was looking over the cell as if something was missing. "That's it!" He turned, looked at one of the officers and said: "Go fetch a couple of extra pillows. We don't want Gene to spend his first day as a paratrooper with a kink in his neck."

Gene took a seat in the armchair as Frank motioned to the remaining officer and ordered him to call down to the *Tic Tac Diner* and order up a full steak dinner for their guest of honor. He told him to make sure they send over one of their cherry pies too. He made it clear to tell the diner they had a "VIP" guest and not to skimp on what he called, "the fixin's." The officer quickly disappeared toward the front of the station.

Frank returned his attention to Gene and told him to "Just sit back and relax while you can, son."

Gene made himself comfortable in the easy chair and replied: "I plan to do just that."

CHAPTER TWO

Camp Grant

The following morning Gene was greeted with a full breakfast, followed by a hot shower and a ride in a squad car to the main gate of Camp Grant—his first journey in a police car. After thanking Frank for the lift, he jumped out of the car and bee-lined for the guard shack at the camp entrance, where he was greeted by a dour-faced corporal, who would prove to be the basis of his dislike for non-coms.

"What the hell kind of trouble-maker are you, Mack?" The corporal's voice was much more high-pitched than he anticipated, especially considering the corporal looked old enough to have served in the Great War. At first Gene was taken aback but quickly recovered.

"Oh, you mean my ride. I played it safe and got here yesterday. There was no way I was going to report late and I needed a place to spend the night so they took me in."

The corporal gave him a quick once-over, shrugged his shoulders, reached into the guard shack, and pulled out a clipboard. He took the orders from Gene and without looking at them said: "Okay, kid. What's your name?"

He provided his name and was further queried for his date of birth, the name of his recruiting officer, his father's name, and the name of his high school. Gene wondered if everyone was subjected to so many questions or if the corporal was simply giving him a hard time. He assumed it was the latter.

Eventually the corporal was satisfied with the fact he was facing Gene Metcalfe, returned the orders, and directed him to a building just inside

Camp Grant during World War II.

the gate where Gene was to report for duty. As he walked away, Gene paused and looked back at the corporal. Another recruit approached him and was quickly ushered through the gate, confirming Gene's suspicions.

Camp Grant served as a "Reception Center," where Gene was only one out of the hundreds of thousands of recruits who would experience their first taste of military life there. It was also a training center for Military Police, firefighters, medical personnel, and, eventually, also served as a prisoner-of-war (POW) camp. Most new recruits would find themselves spending only three days at the camp before being assigned to their respective units. Gene would spend four days there. It would be a harbinger of a string of delays he'd experience with the Army.

A couple hours later, as Gene was standing in line waiting to be issued his uniform and clothing, he noticed a large sign exclaiming: "Look your best as appearance is important." Another sign set forth the description and quantity of every piece of clothing he was to receive, right down to "three neckties." He didn't much like the notion of appearance being so important but decided he'd do what he had to do so he could become a paratrooper. He was singularly focused on graduating Parachute School and reasoned if he had to dress up a bit, he'd do it.

It took about two hours for Gene to finally reach a large window where a few sour-puss sergeants were roughly passing out each recruit's stack of clothing. When he was handed his assigned stack, which included a pair of large, shiny black shoes, he was firmly advised to: "Take good care of this stuff; it's got to last ya, kid!"

Later in the afternoon Gene was undergoing a mandatory medical exam. Though he was in excellent physical condition the doctor was unhappy about his blood pressure. He decided it was too high and announced he was going to discharge Gene, making him ineligible for service in the military. Gene explained he always seemed to have high blood pressure, which didn't appear to impress the doctor. After considering Gene's continued argument, he decided to keep him in the hospital overnight and revisit the blood pressure issue in the morning.

First thing in the morning the doctor returned and measured his blood pressure again; it was still too high. In a matter-of-fact voice he informed Gene he couldn't serve in the armed forces, which sent Gene's mind into a panicked overdrive.

"Doc, what sense does it make to send me back to high school when we need every man we can get?" He didn't stop there. "I played every sport we had and never once had a problem. My blood pressure's not too high for me. Look at me. Have you seen anyone in better shape than I am this whole entire month?"

The doctor took off his thick-rimmed black eyeglasses and held them up for inspection as his forehead furrowed into a series of deep wrinkles. He pulled a handkerchief from his pants pocket, polished the lenses, and put the glasses back on. After taking a deep breath he replied: "Oh alright, I'll let you move on. But mind you, they'll just raise this issue again at Parachute School."

"Doc, that's good enough for me. Thanks!" Gene gave him a salute and very quickly exited the hospital as he feared the doctor might change his mind.

Gene spent the following three days submitting to eye exams, aptitude tests, drills, and various initiations into the "do's and don'ts" of military protocol. He was also the butt-end of a prank one afternoon when he threw himself onto his bunk, only to discover, much to his surprise and dismay, someone had filled it with rocks. When he managed to roll himself out of the lumpy cot he noticed Joey Stickewicz was laughing the hardest among the recruits who had gathered around him.

Standing, Gene said: "Yeah, yeah, I guess I deserved that." He smiled, though he was the subject of the prank.

"Consider us even for that damned cartoon you drew of me!" Stickewicz exclaimed as he promptly walked out, pretending to be upset.

Gene had been referring to him as "Joey the Stick," referencing his slender build, and circulated a comic strip he sketched featuring Joey as a stick figure. It would not be the last time Gene would draw attention as a result of one of his comic strips. Though still a teenager, he had already formulated a firm belief that humor was an essential part of life, even should it occasionally land him in a little hot water or a bed full of rocks.

He quickly developed an appreciation for military routine and also enjoyed the food, though most of his fellow recruits found it very bland. A lover of team sports, he likened the men in his outfit to teammates. In his opinion, it was only a matter of being part of a larger team than he had ever played with in the past.

However, he was following a different career path than most of the men at Camp Grant as he was singularly focused on joining the 508th, no matter what. No infantry, police regiment or medical unit for him. The only road he was interested in following was the one leading him to Parachute School and jumping out of airplanes.

After completing the program at Camp Grant over the course of four days, he was under the impression the Army was putting him on a train to Fort Benning, Georgia, where the Parachute School was located. He was mistaken. As it developed, Camp Toccoa, Georgia, was his next stop, where he joined the newly forming 501st Paratroop Infantry Regiment. Gene arrived the day following the regiment's formal activation on November 15, 1942. He rationalized: "It's not the 508th but it's still a parachute regiment."

CHAPTER THREE

Camp Toccoa

Camp Toccoa was where Gene hoped to begin work toward eventually earning his diploma from Parachute School. As the doctor at Fort Grant predicted, the examining physician at Camp Toccoa also determined his blood pressure was too high. Faced with a medical discharge, Gene, once again, stated his case. He pointed out it was November 1942, Hitler had a firm grip on Europe, and the United States was in a do-or-die struggle with the Japanese on an island by the name of Guadalcanal, and had been since August. He argued: "The Army needs every man it can get." His argument proved to be persuasive; after spending his first night in the Camp Toccoa hospital he was granted medical clearance to join his regiment. It was the same day he received the first of what would prove to be scores of letters from Betty, who tenaciously clung to the hope they had a future together.

Gene wasn't much for writing but did send her, and his parents, the occasional postcard or letter. He had never been particularly adept at expressing himself with words and preferred to convey his thoughts by relying upon art as his medium for self-expression. Consequently, each postcard and letter contained a pen, or pencil, sketch as a supplement for words.

Though Gene had signed up to join the 508th Parachute Regiment, he found himself reassigned. Whether the reassignment was in error or intentional, he never would know. The 501st Parachute Infantry Regiment, 82nd Airborne, at Camp Toccoa was, at a minimum, his temporary home. He soon learned formal parachute training would take

Camp Toccoa, Georgia.

place at Fort Benning, as Toccoa lacked an appropriate airstrip. Toccoa was simply a necessary first step toward earning his diploma.

Part of the training routine included a 5-mile march each day, sometimes taking them past the Toccoa Casket Company, which Gene found to be a little disconcerting. Camp Toccoa had originally been named "Camp Robert Tombs," after a Confederate General. A quick-thinking commander thought it best to disassociate the camp from mental images of caskets and tombs and ordered a name change from "Tombs" to "Toccoa," a reference to the nearby town of Toccoa, Georgia.

The near-daily 5-mile march was barely a warm-up. A particularly strenuous part of the conditioning regimen included a 6-mile round-trip run to the summit of Currahee Mountain. Thanks to his sports background and overall excellent physical condition, Gene didn't think much of the run, though many of his fellow recruits would strongly disagree.

The commander of the 501st was Colonel Howard Johnson. His peers called him by his nickname, "Skeets," though nobody seemed to know how he had acquired the moniker. Johnson was an Annapolis graduate, having transferred to the Army following graduation, and was known as being a hard-nosed, no-nonsense officer with a flair for the dramatic. He put himself in the forefront of the training exercises. Gene and his

Colonel Howard "Skeets" Johnson was killed in combat during post-Operation Market Garden engagements.

fellow paratroopers loved him. Johnson set the tone for the months to follow and Gene considered himself lucky to be a part of his command, even though he generally had little use for officers.

Being a member of an airborne infantry regiment required, as part of the training, becoming expert marksmen. The problem was Camp Toccoa lacked a rifle range. Consequently, Gene and his platoon would routinely embark on 30-mile, each way, hikes to the rifle range at Clemson Agricultural College for extended instruction. Gene soon proved to be the best marksman in the battalion and caught the eye of his sergeant who, unbeknownst to Gene, had him under consideration for an elevation in rank to serve as his corporal.

Gene considered hand-grenade training to be the most dangerous exercise. There was a series of hand-grenade training "pits" dug out and strung in a long row across an open field. Each pit was assigned an instructor/sergeant tasked with the unenviable assignment of teaching recruits how to properly and safely throw a hand grenade. It was a three-part motion.

The sergeant would be waiting in the bottom of the pit for the next recruit to scurry down into the pit with him. He'd instruct the recruit to grasp the grenade in the palm of his throwing hand. The second order was to "pull the pin" while keeping a firm grasp on the handle. Letting go of the handle would trigger about a 10-second fuse, after which the

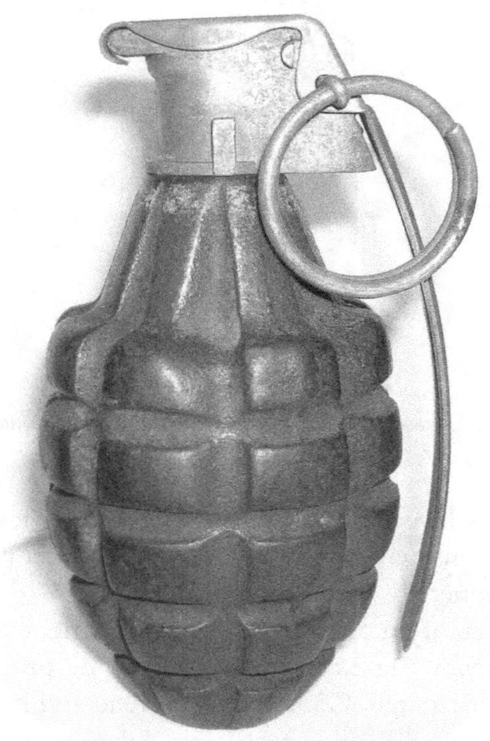

An American World War II hand grenade. Pull the pin while grasping the handle, prepare to throw, release the handle, and throw.

grenade would explode with intentionally lethal consequences. Once the pin was pulled he'd yell out: "Prepare to throw!" The trainee would release the handle, pull his arm back, and the sergeant would immediately shout: "Throw!"

The procedure was simple enough when written into the training manual. A nervous trainee would sometimes let go of the grenade at the same moment he opened his hand to release the handle, causing the lethal grenade to fall to the bottom of the pit. The mistake would immediately send the sergeant and the trainee scrambling over the sides and hitting the dirt as the grenade exploded. Both men would experience a "dirt shower" and try again until it became second nature. Everything the would–be paratroopers learned had to become second nature as their lives would depend upon it.

Training at Fort Toccoa was nearing completion and Gene was looking forward to moving on to Fort Benning for intensive parachute training and graduation from the Parachute School located there. Unfortunately, his military career was about to be inadvertently side-tracked.

On a Sunday afternoon the camp was nearly deserted as most everyone had been granted a weekend pass. After all, their time at Toccoa was ending and most of the men had sought out a little relief before what they referred to as "the real training" began at Fort Benning. Gene didn't have anywhere to go so he hung around the barracks and was in the showers doing his laundry. In fact, he was nearly finished and was rinsing the soap from his fatigues when a newly promoted corporal Gene referred to as "Big Stoop," a reference as much to his brain power as it was to his surname, poked his nose through the doorway and called out to Gene: "I need y'all to get yourself over to the Orderly Room, check out the machine gun and clean it." Big Stoop's southern-accented tone was matter-of-fact and didn't convey any urgency. After all, it was a laid-back Sunday afternoon on a near-deserted training base and Gene was likely the only man he could find to order around.

Gene replied, also in a matter-of fact tone of voice: "Okay, just let me finish rinsing the soap out of my coveralls."

Big Stoop stood still for a moment, staring at Gene, then disappeared.

Gene reasoned the machine gun wasn't going anywhere and knew full well he couldn't just leave his laundry lying around without repercussions. On the second day of camp he'd learned the hard way that the slogan "neatness counts" was a set-in-stone fact of military life so he was not about to leave half-washed laundry sitting out in the open for some officer to stumble upon. He cringed at the memory of being assigned a week of Kitchen Police duty simply for leaving his clean laundry on top of his bunk, instead of being properly stowed away and wasn't about to make a similar mistake.

He had just finished hanging his fatigues up to dry when Big Stoop returned and again, in a matter-of-fact tone, said: "Metcalfe, y'all's wanted in the Orderly Room." He didn't wait for an answer and disappeared.

In a few minutes Gene arrived at the Orderly Room to discover Big Stoop and a "90-day wonder" second lieutenant he knew to be still fighting the Civil War, along with two Military Police, were waiting for him. In a heavy southern drawl the lieutenant asked: "Is this here the felon y'all told me about?"

Big Stoop replied: "He sure as hell is!"

The lieutenant walked to within about a foot of Gene, who was both shocked and perplexed. He barked out: "Y'all was ordered to check out a machine gun and clean it!" He paused as he angrily stared Gene directly in the eyes, having moved within inches of Gene's face.

"Y'all failed to show up and in my book that's insubordination!"

"Oh? What's that?" Gene was not being sarcastic. All the fuss had taken him completely by surprise, and he was thinking this is exactly the kind of trouble he'd been trying to avoid when he made the decision to finish his laundry first, before going to the Orderly Room to fetch the machine gun.

The lieutenant backed off a couple of steps when he recognized Gene didn't possess a southern accent, almost as if Gene might be contagious. He looked him over from head-to-toe with clear disdain and said: "Y'all's disobeyed a direct order and in my book that's insubordination. Y'all's either dumber than a load of bricks or y'all's insubordinate and y'all's can't be that dumb! Report here first thing tomorrow and bring y'all's belongins' with ya!"

The following morning Gene reported to the Orderly Room to find several soldiers standing around, duffel bags in tow. He asked them what they were doing there and they told him they'd had enough. All of them had quit the paratroopers and were shipping out to other regiments. When he asked them where they were shipping off to nobody had an answer other than "anywhere but here." They simply wanted out of the paratroopers and didn't care where they were going or what they'd be doing.

Sergeant De Salvo, his platoon sergeant, walked into the room, noticed Gene's duffel bag and appeared puzzled. De Salvo was known to be a stern yet fair man. He was also a southerner who, in Gene's opinion, was no longer fighting the Civil War.

"Metcalfe, what the hell's goin' on here? Why weren't y'all at roll call?" he demanded.

"Well Sarge, Big Stoop got me kicked out of the regiment and I think they're sending me off to repeat basic training." He proceeded to explain what had happened, which fairly well enraged De Salvo who, still unbeknownst to Gene, was on that very same day going to request he be promoted to act as his corporal.

"Come on, we're going to the captain!" De Salvo was so mad his face had turned beet red.

About 30 minutes later Gene, De Salvo, Big Stoop, and the young second lieutenant found themselves standing before their unit's captain.

De Salvo pled his case and stated Gene was an important member of his squad and he intended to promote him to serve as his corporal. De Salvo pointed out the relative pettiness of the circumstances, reiterating the fact Gene was completely unaware he was being "insubordinate" and in fact wasn't even familiar with the term.

Gene is all smiles as he poses at the top of Currahee Mountain on a Sunday morning in early 1943.

"How could he be guilty of doing something he didn't even know he was doing?" De Salvo exclaimed.

The young second lieutenant proved to be more ticked-off than Big Stoop and refused to back down. It was February 1943, and instead of shipping off to Fort Benning for parachute training he was forced to repeat basic training. His new home would be at Fort McClellan, Alabama.

What he didn't know at the time was that the punitive action taken against him by Big Stoop and the young second lieutenant would keep him out of future action in North Africa, Italy, and France. Perhaps by delaying his training they inadvertently saved his life.

CHAPTER FOUR

Fort McClellan and Buffalo, New York

Fort McClellan specialized in the basic training of new recruits, most of whom were draftees. A person arriving there in early 1943 was facing nine weeks of regimented training, including such activities as vigorous physical workouts, combat training in simulated urban areas, live artillery fire, digging and fighting from foxholes, engagements with tanks, and more. Surrounded by reluctant draftees and naïve recruits, Gene considered Fort McClellan to be a million miles away from Fort Benning and Paratroop School. The singularly focused Gene found himself feeling much like a fish out of water.

Gene was already in great physical condition and discovered the training regimen was relatively easy. In fact, it was much easier than his previous training had been. He was often annoyed by many of his fellow soldiers who were experiencing Army life for the first time. They complained about everything and questioned the need to immediately do as they were ordered. The problem with them, as far as Gene was concerned, was they were overwhelmingly draftees, not volunteers like Gene. He considered the draftees to be lacking in both enthusiasm and self-discipline.

Despite being surrounded by what Gene considered to be slackers, he was trying hard to strictly "toe the line" as he sought to blend into the masses, not draw attention to himself, and make the best of the situation. In short, he had to refrain from doing most of the things which came naturally to him, including the creation of comic strips directing attention to non-coms and officers.

He desperately desired a reassignment to the paratroops, be it the 508th, 504th or 501st. He no longer cared where he wound up, as long as it was a parachute regiment. It hurt all the more when he discovered the movie *Parachute Brigade* was playing in one of the base theaters. When he noticed the poster announcing the movie would be playing all week it reminded him of a time about two years earlier when he took Betty to see the movie back in DeKalb. He felt no closer to being a paratrooper than he did in 1941.

In the early days of his assignment to Fort McClellan, Gene would occasionally wander into the local town of Anniston, Alabama. He was easy to get along with and whenever he saw a piano he'd sit down and begin playing. As a result he was instantly popular with the locals. Free food was the norm. Fort McClellan was also home to ball fields and five movie theaters, so there was always some manner of recreational activity available. Gene believed he was justified in concluding he had it "pretty damn good," at least until such time as he could earn a reassignment to a paratroop regiment.

After about a month had passed, Gene stumbled upon a way to earn an additional 20 dollars a week, which almost doubled his monthly income. Twenty dollars was the going price to take over someone's Kitchen Police duties for the weekend. In his opinion Anniston didn't offer him 20 dollars' worth of entertainment so he maximized the opportunity and became a kitchen fixture on weekends. It also augmented the money he would send to his parents to hold for him until he would eventually return, or spend in the event he didn't make it back alive.

Most of Fort McClellan's full-time cooks lived in town, because they were on long-term assignment to the fort, and parked their cars behind the kitchen. One Sunday afternoon Gene was sitting between some of the garbage cans behind the mess hall taking a break when he noticed a cook poke his head out the door, look around, then duck back in. A few moments later he returned, only he was carrying a 100-pound bag of sugar on his shoulder which he surreptitiously loaded into the trunk of his car.

As he walked back to the kitchen he was whistling a light-hearted tune. The satisfied grin on his face changed the instant he noticed Gene sitting nearby. The cook looked at him and did a double-take.

"Hey, how long have you been sittin' there?" the cook demanded.

"Just a few minutes," Gene nonchalantly replied.

"Listen, come into my office, I want to talk to you." The cook sounded worried.

As they entered the office Gene blurted out he hadn't seen anything. The cook visibly relaxed and explained he had a family and could use a little extra money now and again. Gene again assured him he had seen nothing. The cook stared at him for a few seconds, as if he were deciding what to do, then announced he was making Gene the "Chief of the Kitchen Police," which meant he no longer had any kitchen duties other than overseeing the workers in the kitchen. The title and the extra 20 dollars a week would remain his for the duration of his stay at Fort McClellan. In addition, courtesy of the sugar-thieving cook, he enjoyed steak dinners each weekend.

Gene really didn't break much of a sweat during drills and it wasn't uncommon for him to carry as many as eight rifles, in addition to his own, to help out the men who were struggling. The young and inexperienced second lieutenants thought he was showboating and would put him through various forms of punishment, including sit-ups, push-ups and Kitchen Police duty. Of course they didn't know about his arrangement with the cook.

On one occasion he was ordered to run laps around the parade ground while holding his rifle over his head with both hands. He was just beginning his third lap when he was stopped by a captain who asked him what he had done. Gene replied: "Actually Sir, I don't remember."

The captain smiled and responded: "Son, go back to your unit." Gene concluded some officers were "all-right guys."

Not long afterwards the entire regiment was shipped to Fort Niagara, New York, to partake in a multi-regiment rifle range competition. Gene earned first place in the contest and was rewarded with a medal and a three-day pass. The quandary facing Gene was he really didn't have anywhere to go and since he had it pretty good right where he was he decided to spend his leave with the locals in town rather than travel home or to a larger city. He was truly a small-town kid.

The initial nine weeks of training passed and he found himself surrounded by men being deployed to England. Still more time elapsed, and he realized he had become the odd man out because yet another medical doctor was unhappy with his blood pressure. As a consequence he was put on limited duty.

He sought advice from his sergeant and was told if he wanted to get back into a paratroop regiment he'd need to earn it. Willing to do anything, he took the sergeant's advice and volunteered to be transferred into a newly forming Searchlight Battalion in Buffalo, New York. The sergeant advised him just about everybody in the Searchlight Battalion was on limited duty for any one of a variety of reasons. He also told Gene as long as he was in the Army he had a chance to make it to the paratroopers regardless of the limited duty tag he was stuck with. He said: "Do your best and see what happens."

When Gene arrived in New York he was assigned to living quarters in the Buffalo Armory. The facilities and food were better than he had yet experienced and the men weren't even required to perform any physical training because most of them were on limited duty. He considered being a member of the Searchlight Battalion to be "living the life of Riley." The most strenuous activity he encountered was playing for the battalion softball team.

One day he accompanied a few of the men to a matinee performance at Shea's Buffalo Theater. As was customary for the period the movie was preceded by live entertainment. Quite to their surprise they found themselves in an audience largely composed of "bobby-sockers," all of whom began screaming and crying when the band started to play and a skinny young man took center stage and began singing.

Gene looked around at the screaming girls and asked his pal: "Who the heck is this guy?"

"That's Frank Sinatra," his pal shouted. Gene shrugged his shoulders and amused himself by watching the fanatical girls in the audience since he couldn't hear a word Sinatra was singing.

Following three weeks of relative inactivity Gene was shipped about 15 miles north to the outskirts of North Tonawanda, New York, where

Shea's Buffalo Theatre.

the Searchlight Battalion had commenced field training. Gene described it as "just 15 guys in a small barracks in the middle of a farmer's field."

At the new location he learned how to track local air traffic by training in oscilloscopes and searchlights. He spent his spare time playing softball on the camp's diamond. Locals driving by would stop and give Gene and his fellow trainees cakes and cookies. They would also invite the men to dinner. Gene thought: "Wow! What a duty!"

There was little to do during the day as their duty assignments took place after dark. He'd find himself tracking Bell P-39 Airacobras being employed in the training of new pilots as they flew nearby. He would convey the plane's coordinates to the crews manning the searchlights who'd then "light up" the airplane. He became pretty good at tracking and the searchlight operators proved extremely adept at locating the aircraft with their powerful spotlights.

Over time his performance was deemed exceptional and resulted in an offer to remain with the "Skylighters," a Searchlight Regiment set for immediate deployment to Europe. However, at nearly the same time he was presented with an opportunity for reassignment to the paratroopers and attend the parachute training school in Fort Benning, Georgia. You might say he jumped on it. First, he was granted a leave and decided to take the train ride home to DeKalb since he had not returned home in about a year and it was already November 1943.

Upon his return to DeKalb he discovered that Betty was out of town with her family and virtually all of the men in his senior class had since joined the various branches of the armed forces. Consequently, he mingled with the locals in town, who were pleased to buy him meals and drinks. He wore his uniform throughout his leave, having discovered as soon as a bartender saw his uniform drinks were always "on the house."

Gene's father snapped this photo of him (c.1943) at home for the first time since November 1942. His mother is standing in the doorway.

He had yet to see action but the townsfolk loved him and in exchange Gene regaled them with slightly glorified stories of the various training exercises he experienced, mixed in with some piano playing. On occasion he would sketch a quick pencil drawing of an admirer or the immediate surroundings as a souvenir. Sketching people and scenery would prove to be a life-long practice.

While in DeKalb, on an invite from his old science teacher at DeKalb High, he stopped in the teacher's class to present an informal talk about what it took to become a paratrooper. At the end of his talk the spellbound students gave him loud, boisterous applause as parachute technology was completely new to them. One young man, Billy Carey, asked him so many questions the teacher finally had to bring the presentation to an end, because the class had finished.

As Gene walked past the science room on his way to town Billy Carey flung open a window, stuck out his head, and shouted: "I'll catch up with you in Germany Mr. Metcalfe!" Gene smiled and waved back at him, not giving much thought to Billy's prophetic words.

CHAPTER FIVE

Fort Benning/Camp Mackall

In late November 1944 Gene finally found himself as a part of a class training to be paratroopers, though he was not yet assigned to a specific parachute regiment. He had waited since November 1942 for this opportunity and he wasn't going to let anything stop him this time.

He was ecstatic when he realized the 508th was one of the regiments in the camp and was at the beginning of its parachute training engagement at Fort Benning. He felt it might increase his chances of being assigned to the unit he originally enlisted with. In reality, he was actually one of a large number of paratroopers-in-training intended by the Army to serve as replacements for future casualties. He could find himself assigned to any one of the parachute regiments within the 82nd Airborne.

Gene awoke each day to the boom of a cannon, immediately followed by a bugler blowing reveille into the loudspeaker system. A quick-paced march usually followed, after which they were released to the mess hall for breakfast.

He quickly discovered the Army wasted no time in thinning the ranks of those who weren't cut out to jump from airplanes. One of the first challenges presented to the would-be paratroopers was the dreaded bungee cord drop from a 249-foot-tall tower.

Two men would be strapped into a tandem seat, released from the tower and plummet toward the ground while connected to a bungee cord. The first bungee cord bounce would eliminate, in Gene's opinion, approximately one third of the men, mostly due to illness caused by the abrupt bottoming followed immediately by a rapid rise. Some men simply lost their nerve. Failing the bungee cord jump resulted in immediate transfer to an infantry rifle company.

Actual parachute training began by practicing simple tasks, such as jumping from an approximate 42-inch platform to simulate an actual landing. They were taught to use their knees as a springboard which would enable a paratrooper to quickly stand and gather in the cords from his 'chute. They also jumped from a mock-up of a C-47, in a hangar, to simulate real–life situations.

It was all a part of the philosophy of making each paratrooper's actions completely instinctive to the point they would have no need to think about what they were doing at any given place or time. Time to think was a luxury not usually available to a paratrooper dropping behind enemy lines. To achieve the goal, repetition became the daily routine. The Army considered repetitive drills to be the best method for instilling the essential instincts for performing actions most of the men had never before experienced.

Packing the parachute was probably the most critical exercise of their early training. Paratroopers were required to pack their own 'chutes for at least their first five jumps. After about five jumps specialized "packers" would take care of the chore, leaving the men with more time for training.

Each panel of the parachute had to be perfectly folded, as one tangled line could result in a 700-foot plunge to certain death. The numerous lines connecting the silk parachute panels to the back of the 'chute could be confusing; when combined with the additional lines required for the reserve parachute, many men quickly found themselves packing a tangled mess. Again, it was another task to be practiced until each man could just about pack a 'chute blindfolded. Gene was fortunate, for he possessed an innate sense of how things meshed and was meticulous with his packing, often helping instruct men who were having difficulty maintaining all of the lines in their proper sequence.

Prior to experiencing their first "live" jump from an airplane, the men would be lined up on the edge of the Fort's parachute landing area to observe actual jumps being performed. Every now and again a "parachutist," in reality a dummy named Bessie, would appear to jump from a C-47 flying overhead, experience a parachute failure, and fall to

Practice drops from a jump tower at Fort Benning during World War II.

the ground. The shock of watching what they believed to be a man fall to his death was intended to drive home a point: packing their parachutes properly was absolutely critical as their lives depended upon it. More than one paratrooper in training was fooled by Bessie, and it was a lesson well taken by Gene and his platoon-mates.

Freefalling from 249-foot-tall towers while strapped into a parachute was an opportunity to become familiar with controlling, at least to a limited extent, where a paratrooper might ultimately hit the ground. By pulling hard on the riser lines leading from the left and right sides of the backpack, a paratrooper could attempt to avoid obstacles such as ponds, trees, rooftops, and similar objects rapidly coming up below him. Gene discovered the riser lines weren't a lot of help but were better than having no control at all.

A vast field of sandpits had been constructed for use in daylight, live parachute practice. The sandpits were intended as landing zones over which C-47s carrying paratroopers would fly.

While flying in a C-47 Skytrain, the paratroopers would learn to watch a warning light located next to the open hatch. As long as the light was not shining red or green they were to remain seated. When the light changed to red, it was the signal for them to stand, clip the static line from their parachute to the overhead cable, get in line, and be ready to jump. When the light shone green it was time to jump. After considerable practice the procedure became instinctive to most of the men.

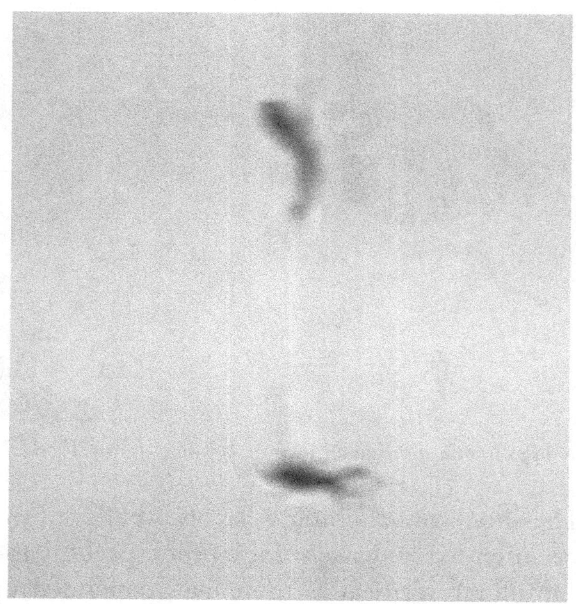

"Bessie" falling to the earth at Fort Benning, Georgia, c.1940.

Once they jumped, manipulating the left and right riser lines would assist the paratroopers in steering themselves toward the sandpits for relatively soft landings. Some men were better at it than others, leaving those who missed the large sandpits to be the butt-end of some practical jokes.

Monday through Thursday mornings Gene's platoon practiced dropping into the sandpits from C–47s, usually flying from between 600 and 900 feet in altitude. They practiced night drops on Fridays. There was an obvious increase in danger when dropping at night, complicated by the fact the Chattahoochee River ran through Fort Benning. While a paratrooper could clearly see the horizon in a night drop, the ground below him was pitch black. Occasionally a paratrooper would unknowingly land in the river and drown when he became tangled in the lines or was engulfed by his own parachute.

While on a night practice jump near the end of parachute training, Gene found himself oscillating. It was hardly unheard of for a circular-shaped parachute to oscillate and was a problem inherent to the design. He found himself uncontrollably swaying back and forth, forward and backward. No matter what he did, he found it impossible to view the ground coming up below him. When he did strike the ground, hard, it was on the backwards motion, ramming the rear of his head into the concrete-like landing area.

He momentarily blacked out, or at least he thought it was momentary. Fortunately, he did regain consciousness before anyone noticed what had happened to him; the fact it was pitch black certainly helped.

His head hurt like hell, he was dizzy, and he vomited. Despite the pain and dizziness, Gene refused to tell anyone about what had occurred for fear it would wash him out of the paratroopers. He reasoned: "I didn't come all this way to be washed out over hitting my dang head. Besides, I stopped in the hospital one day and saw doctors shoving needles up some poor guy's nose and I didn't want anything to do with that."

The dizziness slowly dissipated over the next few days, further justifying his decision to remain quiet about the incident.

Gene and his platoon-mates might spend weekday afternoons packing their parachutes or, after completing five jumps, participating in a wide variety of tactical situation exercises designed to address every potential parachute-landing scenario. The afternoons often featured a forced march covering many miles over a short period of time.

Gene graduated Fort Benning Parachute School on January 8, 1944. At the time Gene considered himself to be the "most over-trained paratrooper in the Army." It bears mentioning the Parachute School was commanded by Brigadier General Ridgely Gaither, an early and ardent proponent of the use of paratroopers. He was also credited with forming the first all-black paratroop unit, the 555th, also known as the "Triple Nickels." General Gaither signed Gene's Parachute School diploma.

From Fort Benning Gene was sent to Camp Mackall, North Carolina. There he underwent additional training in just about every possible aspect of ground fighting imaginable. The simulated battle scenes were intense and would vary from city fighting to forest fighting to open-field fighting and more. They routinely practiced establishing a defensible perimeter around their landing zone in anticipation of real-life battle conditions.

Live-fire drills were incorporated into the training to better simulate actual combat conditions. Occasionally Gene witnessed men lose their nerve under live-fire conditions, the consequence of which could be fatal and always resulted in being washed out of the paratroopers.

The Parachute School
Airborne Command
United States Army

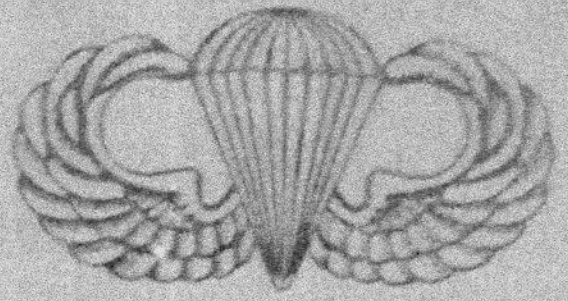

This is to certify that

Pvt.   EUGENE C. METCALFE   16123262

has satisfactorily completed the prescribed course in Parachute Packing, Ground Training, and Jumping from a plane in flight. He is, therefore, rated from this date, _______January 8, 1944_______, as a qualified Parachutist.

Brig. Gen. U.S.A.
Commandant

Gene's Parachute School graduation certificate signed by Brigadier General Ridgely Gaither.

Gene with friends while at Camp Mackall, North Carolina. His pals appear to be admiring his physique. The man second from the right was Paul Pavlis. Pavlis was present at Pearl Harbor on December 7, 1941.

Being a paratrooper required more than possessing the "right" attitude. It also required a paratrooper's body to prove capable of handling extreme and unique physical conditions which could render many men incapable of performing their assignments. Once on the ground, a dizzy paratrooper would likely become a dead paratrooper.

Gene could expect to find himself facing tanks, light artillery, machine-gun emplacements or even snipers. He was trained in just about any battle condition into which he might be inserted.

It was critical to their effectiveness and survival that Gene and his fellow paratroopers prove capable of quickly adjusting to any landing zone situation. Again, the intention was to make fighting in any setting as close to instinctive as possible. A moment's hesitation could be deadly and a paratrooper's instincts could save his life and, perhaps more importantly, the lives of others.

In May 1944 Gene and the balance of his fellow paratroopers were transported to Camp Shanks, New York.

CHAPTER SIX

Camp Shanks—On the Move at Last!

Camp Shanks earned the nickname "Last Stop USA" for the simple reason it literally was the last stop servicemen endured before departing for the European Theater of Operations. The training at Camp Shanks was limited in scope, intended to keep the men sharp and free from serious injuries. Gene was genuinely excited at the imminent prospect of being shipped off to Camp Shanks, for it meant his next stop would most likely be England.

There was a practical purpose for Camp Shanks. At the time, late May 1944, it was a necessary stopover; it was here that all overseas-bound American troops would receive each piece of equipment they might need when engaging in combat. England lacked the proper facilities and supplies to handle the task.

Gene found himself living in a barracks building 20 feet wide by 200 feet long, lined with row upon row of double bunk beds. Though not an issue at the time of year he was stationed there, each building contained only three coal-burning pot-belly stoves for heat. He considered himself lucky it was springtime because he thought the stoves were a rather paltry source for heating such a large building.

It wasn't long before they were put on "alert," indicating they would be shipping out to New York City harbor within 12 hours. Once on "alert," Gene, along with the balance of the troops, was required to remove any unit patches from his sleeves. In addition, he had to mark, with chalk, a specific letter and number on his helmet indicating his marching sequence and train assignment.

It was explained to the men the removal of their Army Airborne and unit patches was for security. The Allies didn't want German spies to learn the nature of the various units arriving in England. They especially didn't want them to become aware of the fact tens of thousands of airborne troops were arriving, as it could tip-off the Germans to expect an invasion from the air.

Gene experienced goosebumps as he made his final preparations and wondered what type of ship would transport him to England. He knew if the ship were a Liberty Ship the crossing could take weeks; if it were a converted ocean liner, the passage might be accomplished in a few days.

He'd never been on the ocean before and was praying he'd be assigned to a fast ship for he had no idea if he'd find himself suffering from seasickness. He'd heard plenty of stories about soldiers, incapable of keeping food down, spending the entire ocean crossing leaning over their ship's rails and heaving their guts out. Just the thought of spending weeks on end, sick to his stomach, was unimaginable.

Upon arriving at New York City harbor, he was excited when he saw the *Queen Mary* and *Queen Elizabeth* docked side by side. Gene was assigned to board the *Queen Elizabeth*, which was slightly shorter and had one smokestack less than the *Queen Mary*. She was, however, newer than the *Queen Mary* and could travel at speeds in excess of 28 knots per hour, making her a nearly impossible-to-hit target for the still dreaded, though no longer particularly effective, German U-boats.

The *Queen Elizabeth* departed New York harbor around May 31, 1944. She sailed without escorts and cruised at a high rate of speed while maintaining a zig-zag course to avoid potentially lurking German U-boats. Sinking the *Queen Elizabeth* with more than 20,000 troops aboard would have made some fortunate U-boat captain a much-decorated man in Germany. While the U-boat menace had been greatly reduced, they remained a genuine danger. For example, on Christmas Eve 1944, the SS *Leopoldville* was torpedoed and sunk by *U-486*, killing 763 of the 2,200 infantrymen aboard.

Gene quickly discovered life aboard the Royal Navy commanded ship was dramatically different, especially with respect to the quality and quantity of food. After nearly 19 months of being fed three meals a day, he discovered the British only provided two meals each day. Aggravating matters further, the quality of the food was far below what Gene had grown accustomed to eating. If he sought to supplement his meals from the canteen, he quickly realized the "Brits" were charging an outrageous 50 cents for a standard-size Hershey's chocolate bar.

Between the bad food, the high canteen prices, and the extremely tight quarters, tensions between the Americans and the British crew ran a little high. Due to overcrowding the Americans were required to sleep in eight-hour shifts. Gene and his fellow paratroopers were not provided a choice of sleeping time. Instead, they were given assigned sleeping times, like it or not.

When not sleeping, Gene would spend the remaining 16 hours of the day seeking out hard-to-find sitting space on the main deck. The converted luxury liner was never intended to house 20,000 or more troops. Even life on deck was somewhat claustrophobic. Personal space was impossible either below decks or topside. It was cold, humid, and the seas were rough, which, when combined with the high rate of speed, resulted in sometimes dramatically swaying decks. Seasickness was rampant. Lucky for him the illness was not a problem.

Amusement, a key element to good morale, came at the expense of the British crew. The ship had been outfitted with 20-millimeter antiaircraft cannons, and watching the Brits attempt target practice turned into good fun. Commencing with the first full day at sea, the crew engaged in target practice. They would launch a weather balloon and attempt to shoot it down. Over a period of four consecutive days of target practice the gunners failed to strike the target even once. Gene thought to himself: "Damn, I hope we don't need them," referring to the antiaircraft gunners.

Fortunately, the Luftwaffe never appeared overhead and around June 4, 1944, they made a stop at Glasgow, Scotland, for fuel. From there they proceeded to Southampton, England, where they disembarked on June 6, 1944, "D-Day."

CHAPTER SEVEN

Nottingham, England

Upon disembarking Gene was delighted to discover he had been designated to join the 508th Parachute Infantry Regiment. He missed the Normandy invasion, having arrived in England on D–Day, and was dispatched directly to Wollaton Park, Nottingham, England. Once there he would await the return of the members of the 508th then engaged in the struggle at Normandy. He was, essentially, a replacement for men killed or wounded in the then-unfolding Normandy campaign.

The encampment was just outside the city of Nottingham and was surrounded by a 10-foot-tall stone wall. Living quarters consisted mostly of pyramid-style tents sleeping four men each, though some tents might house as many as eight. Gene and his best friend, Ray Meade, bunked in the same tent and were practically inseparable. Their personalities were complementary and they did mostly everything together, including occasionally running afoul of their sergeant.

The first few weeks at Nottingham were pretty quiet, with some drills and the usual parachute and equipment maintenance. All of that changed when the members of the 508th who had jumped at Normandy joined the camp. Gene was a bit taken aback at how tired and stressed most of them appeared to be—all except one, the man who was Gene and Meade's new sergeant, Leonard A. Funk, Jr.

Sergeant Funk was probably 8 inches shorter than Gene and built like a Mack truck. He soon made it clear he expected more from Gene, for he had reviewed each man's file and considered Gene to be corporal material. In the opinion of Sergeant Funk, Gene was under obligation to accept promotion. Gene continually confounded Funk with his refusal to cooperate in Funk's quest to promote him.

Gene figured he could barely take care of himself, so how could he be expected to take care of an entire squad? He had never been supported by his parents and had been fairly much on his own when it came to life decisions, even to the point of the elective classes he would choose to take in high school. He lacked the requisite feelings of self-worth he believed were necessary for anyone of rank, even the rank of corporal.

Keenly aware of Funk's intentions, he purposefully approached each exercise just a little too lackadaisically to suit Funk. The reality was Gene didn't need to exert himself very hard in drills as he was in exceptional physical condition and had performed the various drills so often they had become instinctive. It took a concerted effort on Gene's part to give the exercises less than a 100 percent effort as he disdained promotion. He had no desire to find himself in a situation where he might be forced to accept an elevation of his status from private to corporal. He also rationalized to himself that, as he was likely the most over-trained man in the regiment, making a little less effort wouldn't, in the end, make a difference.

Funk also failed to appreciate Gene's sense of humor and was especially riled when he discovered a cartoon strip Gene had sketched depicting Funk in a less than favorable light. Funk never appeared to possess much in the way of a sense of humor while Gene believed, and still believes, humor is essential to maintaining good mental health. His own sense of humor would ultimately prove critical in getting him through the balance of the war. The resulting conflicts with Sergeant Funk caused Gene and Meade to spend many hours mowing a nearby meadow on their hands and knees, using their bayonets as lawn mowers.

The entry gates to the base were manned by sentries whom Gene and Meade made a point of immediately befriending, made easier by the fact they were from their own outfit. It wasn't long before all they needed to do was quickly flash their passes and the sentries would allow both men to come and go without question. The sentries could also count on the two pals dropping off some locally acquired goodies as part of the bargain when they returned.

One day Funk noticed Gene and Meade about to leave the base. He likely figured they were up to no good so he waylaid them and sent both men off to "mow" the meadow. They soon discovered Funk had an uncanny ability to appear from seemingly out of nowhere, despite their best efforts to keep an eye out for him.

Meade managed to get under Funk's skin more than anyone. One day Funk, apparently near his boiling point, ordered him to dig a hole 6 feet wide by 6 feet long by 6 feet deep. When Meade finished, he was directed to turn over his pass to Funk, who tossed it into the bottom of the excavation. He then ordered Meade to fill in the hole. Thereafter, whenever Meade desired to leave the base he would first be required to dig up his pass. The new condition for getting off the base never stopped him. Though the men were generally free to leave the base upon completion of their respective daily duties, Funk always seemed to have a job requiring the help of a couple of privates.

Gene and Meade and a number of the men realized there was an easy way to avoid being snagged by Funk by means of circumventing the main gate altogether. There was a 10-foot-high wall protected by a 6-foot-high loop of barbed wire surrounding the Wollaton Park compound. However, at one out-of-the-way point the barbed wire had been trampled flat, allowing the men to easily scale the wall and save about three blocks of walking in the process. Funk never discovered the alternate exit route.

Gene made many friends in Nottingham and his piano playing caused him to become an instant pub favorite. He was particularly fond of the "Jolly Higglers," where he and Meade became fast friends with Jeff and Molly, a young married couple who lived nearby. The two of them hosted Gene and Meade for dinner on a number of occasions. Gene recalls one in particular with fondness, as he and Meade had provided the bounty for what proved to be a singularly memorable feast.

On a balmy afternoon Gene found himself walking along a gravel track situated behind a series of mess halls for the 1st, 2nd, and 3rd Battalions. As he passed mess hall Number Two a bread truck pulled up to the loading door. The driver mistook Gene as working Kitchen Police and ordered him to retrieve the mess hall keys from the sergeant in charge.

Gene soon returned with the keys and dutifully unloaded the bread truck, except when he was finished with the task he didn't lock the door. Instead, he ran back to the barracks and dumped out his duffel bag. He grabbed Meade, who emptied his own duffel bag, and the two bee-lined for 2nd Battalion's mess hall where they proceeded to load up on bacon, apples, butter, peaches, and canned goods, including meats. If it was edible, they stuffed it into their bags. They dragged the loot back to their barracks and temporarily stowed their bulging duffel bags under their bunks where they could retrieve them later in the day.

Early the same evening, the day's required duties having been satisfied, they threw the duffel bags over their shoulders with the intention of going to Jeff and Molly's for a feast until the sentry on guard at the front gate stopped them.

"What the hell's inside those?" the sentry demanded as he motioned his rifle toward the duffel bags.

"Just our laundry," replied Gene as Meade shook his head in agreement.

The sentry poked at Gene's bag with the tip of his rifle a few times, which produced various metallic "clanking" noises. With a knowing grin on his face he responded: "You two better pick up the pace as it's getting pretty ripe in there." The sentry was a member of their unit so he didn't really care and the two men proceeded to their destination.

Upon arriving at Jeff and Molly's, they poured out their loot into the kitchen, amazing both of them. Molly immediately set to work preparing a dinner, but when she noticed the butter she hid it in a cupboard and said: "The Queen doesn't have butter on her table so neither shall I." While Molly went about preparing their feast Gene played the piano and the three men sang a few songs.

Jeff was home in England because he had been injured in the war and was fulfilling his duty to country by serving as the local air warden. Eventually they would have two daughters, and when Gene tracked down Molly during a return trip to Europe in 1961 he learned Jeff had passed away prematurely. He survived fighting the Germans but didn't live to witness his girls' weddings.

Parachute training continued. Almost every day they practiced situational drops where, upon landing, they would immediately set up a defendable perimeter. It was anticipated they would be deployed behind enemy lines, thus forming and fighting from a perimeter needed to be instinctive. Once on the ground there would be no time for hesitation; each man had to know where to go and what to do without thinking about it. They would be on their own until relief forces could reach them.

One day Lieutenant Weaver, Gene's platoon leader, decided to conduct some bazooka practice. Weaver pointed at Gene and ordered: "You're coming with me."

Weaver had managed to commandeer a Jeep and the two men drove to an abandoned gravel quarry. They disembarked and Weaver pointed to a large rock. "That's your target."

"Sir, I'm not really familiar with how this thing works; maybe we shouldn't use live rounds."

"It's a piece of cake, Private. Take a knee and I'll ram home the rocket."

Gene took a knee, propped the bazooka on his shoulder, and waited for Weaver to tap his helmet, indicating it was set for firing. As soon as Weaver's hand came down on Gene's helmet he pulled the trigger. There was a loud "whoosh," almost immediately followed by an explosion. Gene missed the rock by a wide margin and Weaver was swearing up a storm as the backfire from the rocket nearly burned his arm.

"Give me more of a chance to get away before you fire next time!" Weaver was shaking his left arm as he stared at a small column of gray smoke rising from well beyond the targeted rock.

Though Gene had cause to question how much common sense Weaver possessed, he apparently did possess enough of it to call off further bazooka practice.

Gene and Meade never ventured into London, as they wanted nothing to do with the German V-1, and later, V-2 rocket-bombs routinely dropping into the city. Neither was keen to get, in Gene's words, "blown up," and they were perfectly content to stay close to their base. Other paratroopers would urge Gene and Meade to travel to London with them on their excursions seeking dates, drinking, and dancing. The image of sudden death raining down from above was more than enough to keep them safely in Nottingham where they had no problem meeting ladies and there were no German vengeance weapons to contend with.

One sunny day Gene was participating in a march on the parade grounds when a P-51 Mustang fighter plane made several lazy circles overhead. In itself it was not an unusual sight, for each afternoon, as P–51s returned from their sorties, they would fly fast and low over the base, rocking their wings. It was a signal their mission had been a successful one. Some pilots would flip their planes over, indicating they had notched a "kill." While Gene often made a point of waving at them he considered this P–51's presence to have been "a bit odd." It was too early in the day for the plane to be returning from a sortie.

He didn't give it any further thought until the next afternoon, when he learned the P–51 had been previously captured by the Germans. It was piloted by a Luftwaffe pilot who could easily have shot up the base if he had desired to do so. During Berlin's afternoon radio broadcast hosted by the woman the troops referred to as "Axis Sally," she extended her greetings to "all the men of the 508th Paratroop Regiment." She also expressed her hope they had performed "a nice parade" the prior morning. The episode caused Gene to consider not all things were necessarily as they appeared. It also underscored for him the reality German spies must be in Nottingham, for how else could "Axis Sally" have known detailed information about his regiment and its officers, several of whom she greeted by name during her broadcast?

It was early in September 1944 and Gene asked a local girl for a date. She responded in a way Gene considered to be odd. She told him: "Better make it sooner than that because you're not going to be here Yank; you're going to be in Holland!" Gene had no clue what she was talking about and decided she must be joking. However, it quickly became apparent just about all of the locals were of the opinion Gene's outfit was going to Holland, causing him to wonder if they really did know something he didn't.

A day or two following the P–51's fly-by Gene suffered a leg injury as the result of a hard parachute landing and was ordered into a nearby hospital for recuperation and rehabilitation. After he'd been in the hospital more than a week, Gene decided to follow the doctor's orders to "get in some walking." It was a cool, sunny afternoon when he used the pass issued to him by the hospital and traveled to his base at Nottingham. He couldn't think of a better way to follow the orders than spending some time with Meade, Jeff, and Molly. Intending to locate Meade first, he strolled casually into the camp. He could not know the timing of his walk would forever alter his life.

He noticed Funk was nearly running and was about 50 feet from the intersection of their respective sidewalks. When Funk spotted Gene he abruptly stopped and called out: "Metcalfe! Get over here!"

Gene didn't speed up, as Funk impatiently waited for him. After all, he was recovering from a leg injury.

"Hi Sarge, what's up?"

Funk reached up, placed his right hand firmly on Gene's left shoulder, and announced: "You're coming with me." He paused and pointed in the direction of the Orderly Room. "I know there's an old rifle just inside the entry to that room. Go in there, grab it, and bring it back with you."

"Sure Sarge," replied Gene as he quickly walked to the Orderly Room, poked his head inside the doorway, and noticed a very well-used rifle leaning up against a wall. There was nobody present to stop him so he picked it up. As he took his first step the rear gunsight fell off. Gene shook his head in disgust. When he reinstalled the gunsight he realized its teeth were worn out, making adjustments for wind and elevation practically impossible. He returned to Funk who was barely containing his impatience.

Funk advised him they were going to jump Sunday and Gene had to catch up with "the program." Funk explained he was assembling a 20-man platoon to serve as the first combat patrol going against the road bridge in Nijmegen. He wanted the squad to form up on Gene when they hit the ground. He ordered: "So get to your barracks, find your platoon, and get yourself caught up 'cause you've missed a week's worth of briefings."

"Sarge, where's Nijmegen?" Gene mispronounced the name but Funk paid no attention.

"Holland. Now get a move on private! I'll be around later." Funk hurried on his way and didn't hear Gene say: "But won't I be AWOL from the hospital?" Getting no response from Funk, he shrugged his shoulders and made his way over to his platoon, beat-up rifle in hand.

Meade was happy to see him return from sick leave and did all he could to bring Gene up to date for the planned Sunday afternoon jump into

This M-1 variant was similar to Gene's rifle. The folding stock made it more compact and could be fired with the stock folded as a paratrooper floated to earth.

Holland. Gene didn't like the idea of launching a major campaign on a Sunday, let alone more than halfway through the day. There was going to be no moonlight for night operations, and by the time they landed half the day's sunlight hours would be gone. In any event, he had no choice so he buckled down to the business at hand. Among other things, he still needed to clean his rifle, a gun he was not even sure could be fired.

Later in the evening, when he finally had the time to work on his rifle, he realized the entire trigger housing group had fallen off somewhere between where he had left Sergeant Funk earlier in the afternoon and his tent. He had no choice but to grab a flashlight and retrace his steps along the dusty dirt road until he found it.

Between the gunsight and trigger housing issues he wondered aloud whether "this damned thing will even fire." He couldn't help but continue to worry about the choice of Sunday to kick-off the offensive; it somehow struck him as bad timing, a feeling in his gut he couldn't shake off. He did his best to reassure himself the operation would be okay since everyone was in very high spirits, the Brits in particular.

CHAPTER EIGHT

Operation *Market Garden*

Sunday morning, September 17, 1944, was sunny and fairly cloudless. For security reasons the entire regiment had been encamped in an aircraft hangar, all leaves and passes having been canceled. The mess hall staff outdid themselves preparing what was, in Gene's words, "a huge breakfast." He considered the extravagant meal to be a sure sign they'd be in for a long day.

About halfway through breakfast he realized he knew nothing about Holland or its terrain. All he could visualize were dikes, windmills, and people wearing wooden shoes. His lack of knowledge caused him to feel a bit on edge as he found himself wishing Funk had pulled him from the hospital a few days earlier. If Funk had done so he would have had the benefit of full mission briefings. He felt he was operating at a distinct disadvantage from the rest of the regiment.

Despite his lack of mission briefings he was completely confident in his God-given ability to quickly adapt to changing situations. He also found some comfort in the thought that, as possibly the most overly trained paratrooper in the entire 508th Parachute Infantry Regiment, he would be up to any challenge awaiting him.

Sitting on the top of a three-level bunkbed, he was writing a letter home when he paused and took a look around the hangar, where he noticed three separate religious ceremonies in progress: Catholic, Protestant, and Jewish. The men sitting around each service were calmly cleaning their rifles, sharpening their bayonets or checking their equipment, but not necessarily paying attention to the religious proceedings. He considered it to be an odd mix of spiritual and practical, a scene he would always remember as being singularly unique.

As he slowly looked around the hangar he couldn't help but wonder how many of them would still be alive come sunset, let alone the following morning.

It wasn't going to be a long flight to Holland, and with a jump time of 1330 hours there was ample time after breakfast to speculate, review maps, check his equipment one final time, and relax a little. After giving it some thought he decided it would be a good idea to stuff a few additional grenades into each of his pants pockets. To prevent the wind from sucking the grenades out of his pockets while parachuting to earth he wrapped tape around each leg, right across the pockets. He could easily remove the tape once he was safely on the ground.

In the back of his mind he was hoping no Germans would surrender to them, as the scuttlebutt was to the effect they were under orders to take no prisoners. The order made sense to him as there were only 20 men in his combat patrol, plus a Dutch guide. They could ill afford to send anyone back to the landing zone simply to escort prisoners when they would likely need every man available to accomplish their mission. He had just vanquished the thought from his mind when the hangar doors suddenly opened and it was time to form up.

When Gene marched out of the hangar, he was amazed at the sheer number of C-47 troop transport planes and gliders parked all over the airfield. He found it comforting to see he'd have, in his words, "a ton of company" once he was on the ground in Holland. He allowed himself to relax a little.

With respect to the drop at Nijmegen, he had learned there were two bridges across the wide and rapidly flowing River Waal. One of the bridges was a railway bridge and of no concern to his unit. The second bridge was their objective. It was a fairly new and modern road bridge capable of carrying heavy truck and tank traffic straight up the road leading to Arnhem, the most northerly objective of Operation *Market Garden.*

Gene was to serve as a member of the first combat patrol to reconnoiter the critically important road bridge. He understood it was absolutely paramount the road bridge be captured intact or the entire operation could fail and the war drag on another year.

Once on the ground, Gene, being the last to jump and the last to land, would be easy for the men to spot. The patrol would form up on him and the plan was they were to proceed immediately against the road bridge. Their instructions were clear: avoid engagement, don't stop to take prisoners, seek out the river, and follow it until they reached the bridge.

Their primary goal was to discreetly determine what resistance might be expected and immediately report back to the landing zone. While it was only a remote likelihood they would find themselves in a position where they could seize the bridge, the possibility was not ruled out, as the commanding generals appeared convinced the opposition would consist solely of old men and kids. It was not at all anticipated Gene's patrol might run into tanks or motorized units.

He soon found himself standing in line waiting his turn to board the C-47 transport which would drop him into Holland in the first wave of Operation *Market Garden*. He was the last paratrooper to board the plane and would be the final man to jump. The first men on the plane sat nearest the hatch, while Gene would find himself sitting at the very front of the plane, furthest from the hatch.

Standing in line, anxiously waiting his turn, Gene noticed an American lieutenant positioned alongside the open boarding hatch. He was checking off names as the paratroopers approached him. There was also a British lieutenant standing next to him with a large crate at his side. He was pulling cardboard boxes from the crate and roughly shoving them onto the top of each man's reserve parachute as they boarded.

Gene found himself wondering what the hell could be in those cardboard boxes. He was also questioning why the American lieutenant didn't possess an equipment checklist to verify each man was fully prepared. Instead, the lieutenant's sole focus was in identifying each man as he boarded.

Gene was accustomed to being queried about his ammo supply, rations, gas mask, rifle, the status of his parachute, and the balance of his equipment prior to boarding. This time the officers were only concerned with ascertaining his name and making sure he received one of the cardboard boxes. Since the lieutenants didn't seem to care if they had all of their battle equipment, Gene figured it must be because they weren't anticipating much resistance. As Gene approached the lieutenant and stated his name the Brit pressed one of the unmarked cardboard boxes onto the top of his reserve 'chute. Two of the plane's crew members reached down, grabbed him by his hands and pulled him up and into the cabin. He then took his seat at the very front.

As the men settled into the seats, their backs to the fuselage skin, Gene noticed the guy sitting directly across the aisle had opened his cardboard box. As he removed the contents he started laughing: it contained 144 condoms. He also noticed the windows had been covered with temporary covers, preventing the men from observing what was transpiring outside the plane.

Everyone began opening their cardboard boxes and pulling out the condoms. One paratrooper commented: "The Brits must figure we're in for an easy go of it." Another guy laughingly said the British paratroopers "only got one condom each because that's as much as they could handle." Everyone was having a pretty good laugh when suddenly there was a loud bang. It was the unmistakable sound of an M–1 rifle discharging within the cabin!

Startled, Gene looked at Sam, who was sitting two over from him. Sam dropped to the floor moaning in agony, gripping his right thigh and bleeding profusely. As he rolled back and forth, blood pooling all around him, Gene realized he'd intentionally shot himself directly in the top of his right thigh. Suddenly all the laughter stopped and the plane went quiet, except for Sam's moaning. As they dragged him out of the plane Gene realized the mission had not yet begun and they were already a man short. It was the first time he'd ever seen a man shot and tried not to take it as a bad omen.

In a few minutes they began to taxi toward the runway. Some of the men had blown air into the condoms and were tossing condom balloons out the open hatch. The hatch, by the way, had no door as there was no reason for one. There was no rain in the weather forecast, yet everyone was fitting a condom over the tip of their rifle barrel. The reason was not to keep them dry, but to prevent mud from clogging the barrels when they hit the ground.

Straining to see out the hatch, Gene noticed a number of nurses standing alongside the taxiway were waving at the planes. As Gene's plane rolled past them the condom balloons went flying out the hatch, bouncing down the runway where the wind carried many of them directly into the nurses. They had a sense of humor as not only were they laughing but some of them were picking up the balloons and tossing them at the other nurses.

The condom balloons, and the reaction of the nurses, helped lighten the atmosphere in the cabin, though the trail of blood leading to the hatch was a gruesome reminder of their inauspicious beginning. Gene was struck by how quickly the mood in the plane had changed from jovial, to dead silent and back to laughter. It would prove to be a sequence he'd live through many times over the ensuing eight months.

As the plane began to accelerate Gene instinctively pressed his back against the fuselage. He would have loved to look out a window and silently cursed whoever was responsible for covering them. Since Gene was sitting at the very front of the plane, he couldn't easily see out the hatch and would have felt much more comfortable if he had been able to witness the plane lift away from the ground. He didn't like takeoffs and he'd never experienced a landing; he was a paratrooper, not a pilot.

His plane was among the first to take off. As soon as his pilot established himself as the lead plane in a V-shaped, three-plane formation, he locked in a course for Groesbeek, Holland. The landing zone at Groesbeek was situated on a stretch of meadow-like high ground a little southeast of the city of Nijmegen.

During the prior evening's briefing he had learned the forest on the eastern edge of Groesbeek was in Germany, proper, and very possibly harboring elements of the German Army. He knew if his plane over-shot the landing zone he could be parachuting directly into the hands of the Germans. It then struck him the reason for the daylight jump was likely because accuracy was absolutely critical. He recalled the stories he heard from the Normandy paratroopers of how, in the dark, they landed miles from their intended drop zones, causing them much confusion.

He concluded a daylight jump could be a dual-edged sword and hoped he would be experiencing the dull edge.

For good measure Gene had stuffed as many ammunition clips as would fit into his battle jacket pockets. He reasoned he'd be better off if he were over-prepared than the opposite. He was also carrying more than 70 pounds of mandated equipment plus his rifle. He thought to himself: "No wonder the mess hall cooks went overboard this morning."

All the paratroopers wore "Mae West" life vests over their packs, presumably because they were going to cross the English Channel. Once the men realized the channel was behind them they removed the vests, inflated them, and tossed them out of the plane. At the time it provided a welcome break to the steadily increasing tension. For Gene, it was just one less piece of equipment to worry about and a little less weight to carry. Gene was a practical young man.

There was an iron bar installed above the hatchway door for the men to grab onto before jumping. One of the guys got up, stood at the hatch, grabbed the bar, and began swinging in and out of the plane. Everyone found him amusing, especially when another one of the paratroopers started singing "Rock a Bye Baby." He continued to swing back and forth, in and out, over and over, until suddenly there was a loud noise, much like a large firecracker exploding, followed by a burst of black and white smoke just below him. He swung back in pale as a ghost and returned to his seat. Gene considered the man to have been lucky the antiaircraft burst hadn't blown his nuts off. Just as quickly the laughing and joking stopped and the men grew silent.

Conditions began to get, as Gene recalls, "pretty dicey," as the plane was rocked by a series of nearby explosions, blowing off most of the panels covering the windows. Gene glanced out the window behind him just in time to see a P-51 Mustang whiz by, immediately followed by a plane with a large black and white German cross on the fuselage. "Holy cow," Gene thought to himself; he'd been told the Germans didn't have any fighter planes left and yet there was a Messerschmitt! It was then he began to worry about the kind of overconfidence the Operation *Market Garden* planners must have possessed to produce a decision to issue condoms when maybe extra bazookas would have been in order.

Between the antiaircraft shells exploding above, alongside, and below him, the roar of the engines and the rattling of loose equipment, Gene couldn't think. Nobody was talking; everyone appeared to be too scared. They had all been under the impression they'd be flying into Holland unopposed, and although the weather was clear, the plane was bouncing around as if it had entered a hurricane.

Gene recalled an unsettling story a paratroop instructor related to them back at Fort Benning, about a daytime German paratroop drop in Crete where the German paratroopers suffered such horrendous losses Hitler thereafter banned daylight jumps. Gene tried to shake the image of German paratroopers being shot to death before reaching the ground, but was unable to completely block it from his thoughts.

It was about then he realized he was in a precarious seating position: he was sitting next to a pair of wooden, 200-gallon-capacity spare fuel tanks, each filled with aviation fuel. Gene stared at the twin canisters, and just when he felt he might lose it he got hold of himself and put what he called "the damn fuel tanks" out of his mind. If they blew up there'd have been nothing he could do so he decided not to worry about it. Needless to say, he couldn't wait to jump.

When he next glanced at the ground he realized things were getting worse than they had been told to expect. They were flying at about a 700-foot altitude over Holland and everywhere he looked was flooded, causing him to wish he had not tossed his lifejacket overboard. The flooded fields led him to recall an episode during training at Fort Benning when an unfortunate paratrooper landed in the Chattahoochee River during a night drop and drowned. Gene decided simply to trust his instincts would take over when he needed them and recalled how he once joked he was the best-trained paratrooper in the country for going through training twice. He again realized it was time for his training to kick in so he closed his eyes and pictured himself making a perfect landing, bounding up, pulling in his 'chute and finding himself still in one piece. Feeling more relaxed, he opened his eyes.

The red light alongside the hatch lit up, signaling it was time to get ready. All the men instinctively stood, snapped their static cords to the overhead jump line, and prepared to jump as they'd done many times before. But this was not practice and the antiaircraft shells exploding

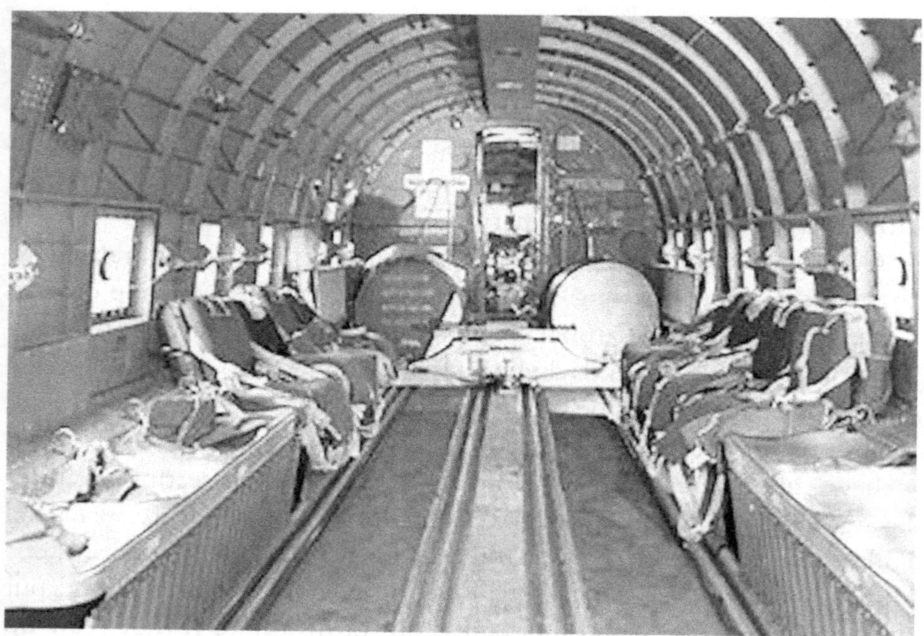

A C-47 could be fitted with up to nine 200-gallon wooden fuel tanks. Under a normal load each engine consumed 50 gallons of fuel an hour, thus the two tanks on Gene's plane extended its flying time by as many as four hours. Rules prohibiting passengers on board while flying with additional cabin fuel tanks were suspended for Operation Market Garden. *This particular aircraft was not configured for paratroop duty. (First Lieutenant Pilot/Instructor and* Market Garden *veteran, Harry E. Watson, USAAF, Ret.)*

outside were very real and uncomfortably accurate. He could see tracer bullets whizzing between the tail of the plane and the open hatch, precisely in the gap through which they would soon be hurdling. He was so scared he could hear his heart beating.

The first man standing in the hatch looked at what was happening below and briefly glanced back inside the plane. It appeared to Gene the paratrooper, a friend of his, was about to vomit. Then the red light switched to green and the jump began. There was no longer time to think and everyone's instincts immediately assumed control.

When it was Gene's turn, though he could hardly swallow, his instincts were in high gear. Without any thought or hesitation, just as had been drilled into him, he moved forward, clasped one hand on either side of the doorway, stepped forward with his right foot, and jumped out,

The tail section from the C-47 of pilot Second Lieutenant Carl A. Cary, shot down while towing a glider packed with paratroopers on the third day of Operation Market Garden. The glider was successfully cut loose before Cary and his crew perished. (Photo courtesy of Robert Cary)

keeping the engine at his back. He was greeted by a sudden silence as he fell away from the plane. No more deafening roar from the motors or the near-misses of antiaircraft explosions. There was only the wind in his face, the sun in his eyes, and the uniquely soft "swish" of bullets whizzing past his head.

He glanced up and noticed the static cords trailing from the door, one for each paratrooper, except for Sam who'd shot himself back on the tarmac. Gene took a final look at his plane and was shocked to see the underside of the left wing in complete tatters. The plane was banking to the right and quickly losing altitude. He watched it continue to descend, its right wing tilting further and further toward the ground, until it disappeared behind a nearby stand of trees.

For a few moments Gene's mind wandered as he was suddenly all by himself, the last man floating to earth. Thoughts of Sergeant Funk again entered his mind. Funk would repeatedly drill into him, although he was part of a fighting unit, each man was alone and each man must perform his role in order for the unit to succeed. As he drifted toward the meadow below he began to form a new appreciation for Sergeant Funk.

He was about a third of the way to the ground when he noticed a German soldier strolling hand-in-hand on a dirt pathway with his girlfriend. The couple suddenly stopped and stared at the paratroopers floating down from the sky. The soldier's body language conveyed shock. He pushed his girlfriend into a nearby ditch and began running as fast as he could toward the cover of a nearby forest. Gene assumed the fleeing boyfriend considered she was safer in the ditch than she was with him.

Glancing around the landing zone, he noticed a German soldier poking his head out from a window in a farmhouse. He was shooting at a sergeant whose parachute was uncontrollably oscillating forwards and backwards. When it would oscillate backwards, the sergeant would fire at the German who was quick to duck back into the house. When the sergeant oscillated forward, the German would poke his head out the window and return fire.

The cat-and-mouse game continued until the sergeant hit the ground. He quickly disengaged from his 'chute, charged the house, tossed a grenade through the window, and rushed inside. Gene wanted to tell him the German had ducked out a back door and was running toward the safety of the neighboring forest but was still in the air himself.

Gene gradually became aware of the fact the meadow he was descending upon was occupied by several German antiaircraft batteries. In addition, each battery was protected by at least two machine-gun emplacements. The antiaircraft guns were situated on the far end of the landing zone and were firing at both the planes and the helpless paratroopers.

The condoms suddenly seemed even more ridiculous and Gene wondered if they were intended to make them relax or whether his generals were that ill-informed. There was no more time for thinking, as he hit the ground with a "whoomp!" He assumed a sitting position, safely below the level where he might get his head shot off by the machine guns, and quickly pulled in his parachute.

They had recently been issued new camouflage-pattern parachutes, and as Gene gathered his in he decided to cut off a few panels to stuff into his pack. He thought the camouflage material might come in handy at some future time, and certainly, if nothing else, it could provide a little extra warmth at night and some good cover. He wrapped one of the panels around his neck to serve as a scarf. As he took a knee and looked around to get his bearings, he noticed several members of his patrol were already making their way toward him.

While the paratroopers jumped with new camouflage-patterned parachutes, equipment bundles utilized either the traditional white parachutes or newly introduced colored parachutes. The color of the parachute indicated the likely contents of the equipment bundle. He couldn't help but notice Mike, his patrol's designated bazooka man, desperately rummaging through one of the equipment bundles and wondered what he could possibly be looking for.

Sergeant Funk, his ever-present Tommy gun slung over his shoulder, suddenly ran up to him, breathing heavily and seriously agitated. Close on his heels was one of Gene's buddies, a man who had recently been busted down from sergeant; reason enough for Gene to be particularly fond of him.

"Metcalfe," Funk was almost shouting, his eyes practically on fire, "you're hooking up with us. We're going to take out those God-damned Nazi guns before they kill any more of my boys!"

"No can do Sarge," Gene responded.

Funk paused and said: "What did you say?" He sounded both incredulous and angry.

Funk shifted his Thompson to his other hand almost as if he intended to throw a punch.

"Sarge, you've got me as the point man on this combat patrol and they're forming up on me right now."

Funk paused as he considered the situation. He obviously wanted Gene with him as he was his best rifleman. The problem he faced was he'd personally chosen Gene to serve as the man around whom the patrol was to form up and he couldn't very well change his choice, post-jump.

"Have you seen Buck or Pete?" Funk asked as he looked around for a substitute.

"No Sarge, I haven't seen 'em."

After a brief pause Funk put his right hand on Gene's left shoulder and said: "Listen, you're the best shot in the outfit and you've got good common sense so take care and I'll catch up with you later." Funk could not know "later" would turn out to be several decades later.

Funk looked around for a replacement and pointed to a couple of paratroopers sitting nearby, both of whom appeared lost. He motioned them over and said: "You guys are coming with me."

Unfortunately, just as one of the paratroopers stepped up to join in with Funk he was shot through the throat and fell backwards, hitting the ground with a sickening thud. Blood gushed from the mortal wound; he looked shocked and unaware of what was happening.

Funk immediately slipped the Tommy gun from his shoulder as his face turned beet red. He began charging toward the nearest German antiaircraft gun position, firing his Tommy gun and yelling like a man gone mad. Funk was fluent in German and was mixing English cuss words with German as he charged ahead, two paratroopers obediently in tow. As it ultimately turned out, one of the accompanying paratroopers went on to become a medical doctor after the war and Funk would become the most decorated paratrooper in United States history.

A German antiaircraft battery in action.

After a few minutes Gene, having taken a knee, heard the first German antiaircraft gun emplacement and the machine guns protecting it go silent. Gene continued watching as Funk, followed by his two accomplices, once again opened fire with his Tommy gun as he recklessly charged the second German installation. Gene heard Funk's Tommy gun firing almost nonstop until all of the German guns were silent. By then Funk was barely visible as Funk had reached the far end of the drop zone. He had just about singlehandedly taken out all three German antiaircraft installations and their protective machine guns.

Gene calculated Funk had killed a minimum of three dozen Germans and permanently silenced the antiaircraft guns. The decoration awarded Funk for his action may have failed to make a complete count of the antiaircraft and machine-gun installations he destroyed. Gene was present and witnessed the event, firsthand. He remembers three installations, not two, as listed on Funk's citation.

CHAPTER NINE

Road to Nijmegen

Around the same time Funk knocked off the last of the antiaircraft gun emplacements, most of the 19-man combat patrol had caught up with Gene. Together they began to work their way toward a point at the far end of the meadow where the main road leading into Nijmegen vanished into a tree line. It appeared to be a defensible position so they established a perimeter and waited for their lieutenant to catch up with them.

In a little while Lieutenant Weaver, their platoon leader, arrived and brought with him a member of the Dutch underground wearing a Dutch Army uniform. They were told he was from the Nijmegen area and very familiar with the landscape. Though unarmed he was to serve as their guide and brought their manpower back to the original 20.

Gene commented to Meade he thought the Dutch uniform bore an unsettling similarity to the uniforms of the German Wehrmacht. Their discussion was cut short when Weaver motioned for the patrol to gather in a semicircle before him.

He explained their objective was to reconnoiter the road bridge, get a handle on the German strength, and report back. He told them it was G-2's opinion the defense would probably comprise elderly home guards and children and if that were true they might just go ahead and take the "damn bridge." He then advised the men that one thing had changed since the night before, as they had new orders redirecting their approach to the bridge. They were going to march straight up the main road, right through Nijmegen, rather than divert easterly to the Waal and follow its banks to the bridge.

He mentioned there'd be a patrol somewhere out on their left flank and another on their right, the latter led by Lieutenant Foley taking over their original route. He said it was unlikely they'd make contact with either so they shouldn't anticipate any assistance in the event they actually ran into trouble. He also mentioned the Dutch underground had reported the Nijmegen post office housed the demolition leads from the bridge. If possible, they were to secure the post office building and disable the detonation equipment.

Weaver looked over his assembled troops, some too young to shave and no one older than about 23, several of them anxiously adjusting their rifle sights, others nervously puffing on cigarettes, and said: "Now this is important, so listen up. If we do run into trouble I don't want anyone to fire a shot unless I say so. I want to take the Nazis by surprise, I repeat, by surprise, and that means don't fire your weapon without my order. Understood?"

He was met by silence. Satisfied, he concluded with: "Colonel Lindquist has ordered us to stay put until further orders, so settle in."

Silence set in amongst the men as they checked their rifles and bided their time awaiting the order to proceed. Gunfire had almost completely died down and the scene was taking on a surrealistically quiet atmosphere.

Around 1800 hours their commanding general, James Gavin, learned the patrol had been ordered to stay put and immediately issued them the order to move out. The patrol finally got underway shortly after 1800 hours, four and a half hours after they had jumped, allowing the Germans plenty of time to begin assembling a defense. Darkness would set in around 2200 hours, yet Weaver set a slow, deliberate pace.

They split into two single-file lines, one on the left side of the road where Gene was assigned and one on the right side of the road where Meade was roughly a couple of yards further back from Gene. They had been taught the resulting staggered pattern to be the best way for a patrol to spread out when following a road or advancing in urban settings.

Initially the road was fairly flat and just barely wide enough to accommodate two-way traffic. In the event the road was mined they were sticking to the rugged roadside, further slowing the patrol's progress.

The road bridge over the River Waal. The once picturesque city of Nijmegen was devastated during the battle to take the bridge.

The surrounding terrain was mostly marsh, with occasional stands of tall weeds potentially providing cover for hidden German machine-gun nests. Gene began to realize each step he took could be his last as he tried to keep an eye on the horizon ahead of him and the surrounding terrain at the same time.

The patrol moved only slightly less deliberately once they determined the Germans probably had not land-mined the road. Around 1930 hours some locals, riding bicycles, approached them from the direction of Nijmegen. They bore huge smiles and were seeking to extend greetings to their liberators. They began passing out apples and bottles of wine but were waylaid by the Dutch guide. He spoke with them only long enough to confirm the road was clear of both land mines and Germans. He ordered the cyclists to take their wine, leave the apples, and go home

This photograph was apparently taken by a member of the patrol during the capture of two elderly German soldiers. The uniformed Dutch guide (third from the left, standing) has his left hand on his belt. To his right is a captured German without a helmet and behind him appears to be an already deceased German, lying back in some type of a cart. The photo appears in Market Garden Nijmegen *by Tim Saunders and appears courtesy of Tim Saunders. What follows is the full story behind the photo. Mike, the bazooka man, is carrying a bag of hand grenades, having left the bazooka rockets on the floor of the plane in his haste to jump.*

right away. He also instructed them to make no mention of seeing any Allied soldiers and to remain indoors at least until morning. Gene wondered how they knew the location of his patrol.

With the cyclists pedaling away at a good clip the patrol proceeded to press forward at what Gene considered to be, at best, a sightseeing pace. After so many forced marches he found it difficult to walk as slowly as they were. It appeared to him as if Weaver considered time was not of the essence.

Shortly after their encounter with the Dutch cyclists, the road opened up with about 10–20 feet of clear area on either side. The flanks of the road harbored 6-foot-tall stands of grass; beyond was forest. The photograph above captures the terrain very well, along with the casual attitude of the detachment.

Suddenly two older German soldiers appeared out of nowhere and stumbled directly into the middle of the patrol. Their emergence alarmed

Gene as he had walked past the pair without spotting them. If it wasn't for the commotion coming from behind him he might never have known. The patrol paused as two paratroopers and the Dutch guide quickly and quietly disarmed the two elderly Germans, members of the Wehrmacht and certainly not "SS."

Gene took a knee and carefully re-scanned the surrounding area in all directions, assuring himself there were no more surprises lurking nearby. The abrupt emergence of the two elderly Germans had left him a little flustered. He glanced across the road and spotted Meade, who had also taken a knee. Meade pointed up the road and in a low voice said, "Don't look back."

In a few minutes Weaver jogged up to Gene and told him to get moving. He was going to take up a position a couple yards behind Gene who was, at that moment, the first man in line on the left side of the roadway. Weaver told Gene to signal him should he notice anything odd up ahead. Gene chose not to ask him about the prisoners and the patrol continued forward at the same slow, deliberate pace.

Following another half-hour of minimal progress, there were no new indications of German activity. There wouldn't be any moon that night but, Germans or not, Weaver had the patrol maintain a slow pace. Soon enough the sky offered only a hint of light beyond what the stars might provide. It wasn't yet total darkness but it was getting close. Gene estimated they were not covering 2 miles an hour and wished they would increase the speed of their advance while they still had at least a minimal semblance of light.

Gene paused and scanned the horizon; it appeared the road was narrowing at a point where it disappeared into the hazy, post-sunset gloom. Gene was nervous because he was aware a narrow road wouldn't leave much wiggle room in a firefight. To make matters worse, they never practiced reconnoitering a constricted road, the likes of which they were about to confront.

The narrowing of the road would prove to be worse than he anticipated. After about a quarter of a mile they discovered the road nijsintegrated into a very tight, sunken road. There were 8-foot-high dirt berms on either side sloping down to the very edges of the roadway, which was barely wide enough to accommodate one-way truck traffic. The prospect of being caught on such a road in near-darkness, in Gene's words, "scared the shit" out of him and likely alarmed everyone else as well.

They had no choice other than to proceed as quickly as feasible into the shadowy, darkened, cavern-like roadway. They didn't dare walk on top of the berms lining the road, as the outlines of their bodies would be silhouetted against the grey sky, making them easy targets. Gene made certain to continuously scan not only the road lying before him, but the tops of the berms as well.

The berms lining the road caused Gene to experience an ever-increasing sense of claustrophobia, aggravated by the fact he had no idea what was on the other side of them. He rationalized they probably kept water from flooding the road, which would keep the Germans off their flanks—at least that's what he hoped was on the other side of the berms. It was quiet, with no discernible breeze. A German could appear at any time.

They had been walking along the sunken road for about 15 minutes when they found themselves roughly a couple hundred feet from an intersection, barely visible in the diminishing light.

The road to Nijmegen ran, more or less, northwesterly to southeasterly, and the approaching crossroad ran east–west. Consequently, when they would cross the pending intersection their silhouettes could easily be spotted by Germans who might be on either side of them. Gene thought it would make good sense for the Germans to hide a machine-gun outpost to guard the intersection, rather than at some random point up the road. To him this presented a perfect opportunity to walk into an ambush.

Suddenly, acting from instinct, Gene stopped. Weaver came up behind him as both men peered into the near total darkness shrouding the intersection ahead.

"Why are you stopping, private?" Weaver whispered.

Before Gene could manage an answer the still air was interrupted by the faint sound of a motor. They turned and looked behind them. Observing no movement, they returned their attention to the looming intersection.

The berms were acting as echo chambers, initially masking the fact the sound was coming from ahead of them and to the left. The noise steadily grew louder; soon Gene and Weaver realized they were listening to a tank in motion. It couldn't be one of theirs for the simple reason they didn't have any tanks.

Weaver remained standing beside Gene when the unmistakable profile of a German Tiger tank pulled across the road and stopped in the center of the intersection. It was less than 100 yards distant. Gene could discern there were white numbers on the turret, which appeared to be an outline of another, darker color; perhaps the centers were red and the outline was white, he thought.

Too scared to spend time worrying about what number was painted on the tank, he was, in his words, "practically shitting" in his trousers. Gene had listened to numerous horror stories about Tiger tanks from the 82nd Airborne Normandy veterans and suddenly there was a Tiger tank right in front of him, blocking the only route leading to the road bridge at Nijmegen.

The entire patrol froze as they stared at the Tiger. Gene wondered which direction it might go—perhaps it would continue east?—but no such luck, as it turned, almost in place, and faced the patrol. Without thinking Gene whispered: "Sir, I doubt he can see us in this light 'cause he's battened down and can only look straight ahead through those little slits." Gene pointed to what appeared to be an observation slit in the front of the Tiger.

"Get the bazooka!" Weaver yelled.

Gene calmly replied: "No can do, Sir. Mike was in such a hurry to jump he left his bag of rockets on the floor of the plane. All he's got in that bag he's carrying is a bunch of hand grenades."

Realizing they had nowhere to run, Weaver motioned for the men to lie back into the berms and wait. Gene and everyone else did the best they could to burrow themselves into the weeds, rifles on their chests, no doubt praying the crew inside of the Tiger wouldn't spot them.

It was only then Gene realized the Dutch guide had disappeared. He wondered if this was a set-up and perhaps the guide was not really a member of the resistance. He considered the fact none of them spoke Dutch and wondered if the locals they ran into earlier had actually forewarned the guide there were Germans in the area. No answer to his question would ever make itself known and there was nothing he could do about it regardless. Still, the timing of his disappearance was unsettling.

The Tiger was approaching very slowly, moving only slightly faster than the casual pace at which they had been proceeding themselves. Gene hadn't yet observed any infantry trailing behind the tank, when suddenly the machine gunner opened fire from the front of the Tiger. Gene pressed himself more deeply into the berm. After a couple of moments he realized the gunner was firing blind, straight up the road, and not spraying bullets side to side. Gene thought to himself, if it were *him* behind the machine gun, he'd be splattering the thing left, right, up and down and was thankful the machine gunner wasn't like him.

The Tiger moved so slowly it reminded Gene of pheasant hunting. When working a field of downed corn while hunting pheasant back in DeKalb he'd walk very slowly, stopping now and again for a few moments at a time. Spotting a pheasant nestled amongst the downed corn stalks was just about impossible, but pheasants would get nervous and flush when their stalkers came to a stop, creating an opportunity for dinner.

It was the same with this Tiger. Every 20 or 30 yards he stopped and waited as the machine gunner splattered a few more rounds up the roadway. It had a near-unnerving effect as the tactic was also effective against the Tiger's human pheasants.

Gene was sure everyone felt as he did and wanted to get the hell out of there, but it would have meant certain death and he wasn't about to become a human pheasant. So Gene pressed his body ever more deeply into the berm and watched and waited with much more patience than the pheasants back home.

Luck seemed to be with them, as there were no soldiers following behind or riding on the tank. The Tiger was a rogue, out on his own, seeking to create a personal hell for some poor souls.

After what felt like hours the Tiger was directly alongside Gene. It was, in his words, "so damn big the tank treads were within two inches of my boots." Even if it had been feasible Gene didn't think he could run. He froze, staring at the Tiger's massive turret as it stopped directly in front of him. The machine gunner let loose a few more bursts into the

A German Mark VI Tiger tank. The machine gun is to the left and the observation port to the right.

darkness before the tank again rumbled forward in the direction of the landing zone. The hot exhaust gases singed his face as it slowly moved past Gene's prone body. To this day he can recall feeling the heat of the exhausts searing his face.

It took nearly 15 minutes for the Tiger to work its way down the road and safely beyond the patrol. Though the Tiger was still audible, the tank was melting into the darkness. The patrol cautiously began to move out as they continued to press forward toward the heart of the city of Nijmegen and the road bridge.

They soon left the claustrophobia of the berm-walled road and found themselves facing a small clearing on the outskirts of Nijmegen, when a runner sent by Colonel Lindquist caught up with them. Word was passed they were to spend the night "in-place" and resume at dawn. They took off their packs and had barely commenced settling in when a second runner from Lindquist arrived and countermanded the prior order. The bivouac lasted less than 30 minutes but the unexplained delay provided the Germans with additional time to organize their defense.

CHAPTER TEN

Keizer Karel Plein

In a matter of minutes they found themselves walking among scattered houses and businesses, an outcrop of the city of Nijmegen. Sensing movement, Gene paused and stared into the near-darkness, straining his eyes trying to determine whether the movement was a man or only a bush reacting to the breeze. Weaver came up alongside him and stared in the same direction.

As if on cue a German armed with a Schmeisser machine pistol, sometimes referred to as a "burp" gun for the sound it makes, stepped out from behind the corner of a building about 50 feet ahead of the two men. Without hesitating, he unleashed his entire 20-round clip directly at them before he quickly disappeared behind the building. Gene and Weaver looked around, realized nobody had been hit, and considered themselves to be lucky. Perhaps the opposition in the area was as ill-trained and unprepared as their commanding generals believed them to be.

Though all was again quiet there was at least one German racing to raise an alarm. Weaver then passed the word: "Fix bayonets!" Gene felt a chill run down his back as he removed his bayonet from its sheath and locked it into his rifle's barrel with a distinctive "click."

It was about 2200 hours and nearing total darkness as they slowly and quietly made their way past darkened houses and storefronts. As the patrol approached a minor intersection they discovered two Germans, one sitting on a motorcycle and the other standing next to him. The two Germans were engaged in quiet conversation and completely unaware of the Americans nearby. Instinctively, Gene raised his rifle to fire when

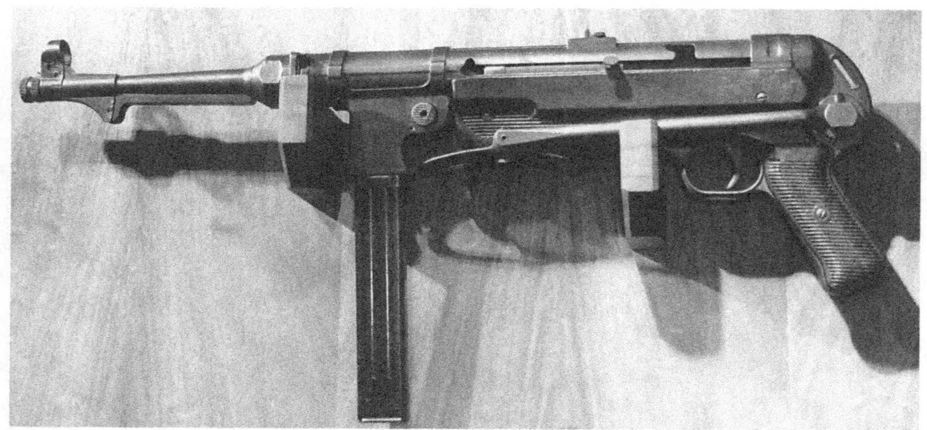

The Schmeisser MP-40 machine pistol was routinely used by German infantry in WWII.

Weaver came up behind him, put his hand on his right shoulder, and whispered: "Don't fire; it'll give us away."

The word was then passed to the entire patrol: "Don't fire!"

Gene looked at the two Germans as they casually turned, glanced over at him, and froze.

"Sir, it appears they already know we're here." He received no reply.

Ignoring the two Germans, the patrol continued to walk past them. Inexplicably the Germans remained frozen in place, except their heads were moving as they followed the progress of the patrol. It was a bizarre experience as neither side fired at the other.

After walking about half a block further, Gene glanced behind him and discovered the two Germans had disappeared, the motorcyclist having dropped his "Beamer" to the ground in his haste to quietly and quickly escape. Gene wished he had followed his instincts and shot them. As he recalls: "I could have knocked them both off in three seconds." Gunfire was probably not unusual around there, and by allowing them to escape the Germans knew precisely how many men were in the patrol and where they were located. Gene's anxiety level notched up a bit, and for good reason.

In a matter of a few minutes, two troop-laden transport trucks, followed by what looked to Gene to be a half-track, rumbled into view. They were on the far edge of a park that had opened up in front of the patrol and were motoring directly at them. They appeared to be coming from the direction of the road bridge which Gene believed couldn't be more than a few blocks away, at most. As they began to enter the park, all three vehicles abruptly stopped. It appeared to Gene that despite the near-dark conditions, they may have been spotted.

Gene knew that just beyond the German transports was a large roundabout where several streets converged from at least six distinct angles. From his memory of the map the roundabout was probably the Keizer Karel Plein. What Gene and his patrol didn't know was the Germans had taken up positions in the center of the Plein, in the buildings surrounding it, as well as in some of the structures along the perimeter of the park. In addition, they had camouflaged among the trees a twin 20-millimeter antiaircraft cannon repositioned for firing at ground targets and a much-dreaded, both for its range and accuracy, 88-millimeter cannon supported by a pair of machine guns.

The park afforded only nominal protective cover in the form of scattered trees, bushes, and precious little else. The trees, however, were mature elms with at least 2-foot-wide trunks. Gene took up a position behind one of the elm trees and peeked around it as the three German vehicles remained in place on the northeasterly edge of the park. At that point he assumed they must have spotted his patrol; otherwise, he thought, "why would they stop?"

If you were to visit Nijmegen today, the trucks would likely have entered the Plein area from the east on Oranjesingel Road, coming to a stop with the park spreading out before them. They would be looking for Gene's patrol, which they no doubt knew was coming into the Plein via Groesbeekseweg Road from the south.

After a short pheasant-hunting pause, the first troop transport began to slowly move forward. There was a hole cut in the steel roof of the cab, above the passenger seat, where a soldier stood manning a mounted machine gun. A wide piece of sloping metal running across the top of the cab afforded the gunner some semblance of protection.

It was impossible for Gene to gauge how many Germans might be in the back of the truck since it was covered with a canvas tarp, but it made sense to him the truck would be full of soldiers. His luck didn't change as the truck came to a rest about 4 feet away from him, directly

The Keizer Karel Plein in Nijmegen, Holland. Parks are to the southwest and southeast of the roundabout. North is at the top of the picture and south is at the bottom. The park, today a concert venue, is the location of the firefight and lies on the southeasterly border of the Plein.

opposite his protective elm. It was a repeat of the move the Tiger tank had employed about an hour earlier. He was so close he could clearly distinguish the facial features of both the machine gunner and the driver, each leaning forward, trying to establish what might be lurking head. Curiously, neither of them looked in Gene's direction.

He slipped around the far side of the tree, took aim at the machine gunner's head and said to himself: "You've got about a second to live, if this rifle works." As Gene squeezed the trigger, all hell broke loose. The truck exploded in a wall of flame and debris, sending the upper half of the machine gunner's torso into the air. Body parts landed on and around Gene and in the tree overhead. Screams pierced the night.

Unbeknownst to Gene, his platoon had advanced at such a slow pace that the patrol off their right flank, led by Lieutenant Foley, had reached the River Waal and were making their way toward the Keizer Karel Plein. They were probably attempting to make contact with Lieutenant Weaver's patrol when they arrived on the edge of the park.

Foley's patrol likely came from the east via Bijleveldsingel Road and possibly found it necessary to divert south and utilize side streets due to German traffic on the main road from the bridge. It was very dark when Foley's patrol reached the park at the same time as Gene's, though from a different direction. Neither patrol was aware of the other, as both were focused on the Germans.

Noticing the troop transport had come to a halt, Foley quickly sized up the situation and brought his two bazooka-men forward. Unaware Gene was positioned just beyond the troop carrier, Foley directed a bazooka volley, which struck the truck at the same moment Gene had been squeezing his rifle's trigger. Gene would never know if his bullet had found its mark before the truck exploded. He erroneously, though understandably, assumed the truck had been hit by hand grenades.

He ignored the explosions and the body parts landing all around him and kept his focus on the burning truck. After firing a few rounds with his rifle, he began lobbing grenades as fast as he could. In fact, both patrols gave it everything they had. In the darkness Gene couldn't be certain whether any of the Germans escaped what had become a furiously blazing inferno. All he knew for certain was one second there had been explosions and all manner of small-arms fire, and then it was dead silent.

The burning truck was lighting up the immediate surroundings, creating awkward shadows and he imagined Germans could be hiding all around him. He was unaware Foley's patrol had joined the engagement and rightfully believed there could have been a German behind any of the nearby elm trees. He remained behind his protective elm and waited to see what would happen next.

As near as he could ascertain, nobody in his patrol was moving and it seemed as if time had been abruptly frozen. No shouts, no orders, no cries for help; everything was perfectly still and eerily silent. Each patrol, still not cognizant of the other, stood its ground.

Almost unbelievably, one of the remaining two trucks began to slowly move forward in the same manner as the first truck. Gene couldn't understand the German thinking, as they were attempting a repeat of the same disastrous tactic. After the patrols blasted the second truck in similar fashion, Gene observed Germans disembarking from the remaining transport.

Though it was dark, Gene recognized the Germans were scattering toward both of his flanks. After a brief lull, the night erupted with a cascade of rifle fire. A German 20-millimeter antiaircraft cannon being employed as a close-range weapon and the much-dreaded 88-millimeter cannon/antiaircraft gun entered the fray.

Tracers crisscrossed the park, seemingly coming from all directions as it was immediately obvious the Germans commanded a definite numerical and firepower advantage. They also possessed the high ground from where they could easily direct their artillery volleys onto the American patrols. There were explosions all around him as Gene considered it to be a scene straight from hell.

What the Americans didn't know was they had come up against the 10th SS Panzer Division, not a bunch of old men and kids. These were among the best the German Army had to offer and they were hellbent on defending the city, and especially, the road bridge.

At some point the order to fall back was given by Lieutenant Weaver. Gene, however, was in a forward position and didn't hear the order. He stood his ground and continued to fire at the Germans as fast as he could, having run out of hand grenades. Meade did hear the order and realized Gene wasn't pulling back. Unwilling to leave his friend, he decided he'd take a chance and charge across the roadway to let him know they were pulling out.

Just as Meade took his first step toward Gene's position, a shell from the German "88" exploded near Gene and threw his body high into the air, hitting the ground with an audible thump. Undaunted, Meade continued across the road, dodging enemy fire the entire time, and found Gene lying face-down. He rolled him over, noticed blood coming from his right ear, and assumed the worst.

Gene was left for dead at Nijmegen, the only member of the patrol who did not return. His status was about to change from "Absent without Leave" (AWOL) to "Killed in Action" (KIA). In a few days, when his body did not turn up and nobody could account for him, following the capture of Nijmegen, his status was changed to "Missing in Action" (MIA).

CHAPTER ELEVEN

Nijmegen

Gene had no idea how long he'd been unconscious; he found himself lying on his back, his helmet nowhere in sight. His head was splitting so badly he thought he'd been struck a direct blow from a hammer and his right ear burned. He felt as if there were weights on top of his legs, locking him into place, and an annoying, loud buzz rang inside his head. He rubbed his cheeks, checking whether his face felt contorted.

When he attempted to stand, a stomach-churning, spinning sensation violently slammed him back into the ground where he decided to remain, eyes pressed shut. He thought if he closed his eyes as hard as he could the spinning sensation might go away. After a few moments he opened them again, only to discover his brain still thought he was on a merry-go-round.

Gene made a couple of attempts to get hold of himself, for he had a bad feeling time was not on his side. He needed his body to cooperate; his hard, back-of-the-head nighttime landing at Fort Benning briefly came to mind. He recognized this injury was worse, much worse than before.

He couldn't figure out why it was so silent and considered the possibility everyone might be dead. Certain there had never been an order to fall back, Gene nevertheless had the unpleasant feeling he was all alone. The unsettling realization his patrol had either disappeared or been wiped out was slowly sinking in. Keeping his eyes closed seemed to ease the headache and the spinning sensation. He purposefully didn't move a muscle, lest he attract unwanted attention, as he thought to himself: "I just need a little time to regain control of my body then I can get the hell outta here."

No more than a few minutes passed when Gene felt something poking into his gut. He opened his eyes and in the darkness realized a German soldier was pressing a rifle into his stomach, checking whether he was alive or dead. Gene's eyes opened wide as he realized his precarious situation. In response, the surprised German immediately backed off a couple of steps and began shouting "Aufstehen! Aufstehen!" while pointing his rifle directly at Gene's torso. Gene didn't know what the term meant but he had a pretty good idea and tried to stand.

It took some effort but Gene made it to his feet, when dizziness again kicked in and his knees buckled beneath him. The German grabbed his arm and helped hold him upright. Gene put his hand to his right ear and felt a sticky liquid; he realized he was bleeding and assumed he'd been shot though he didn't feel as if he'd taken a bullet. The very loud buzzing in his ear made hearing difficult and contributed to the feeling of being disconnected from reality.

He momentarily considered the possibility he was dreaming, or worse yet, dead. Feeling the ground beneath his boots and the grip of his German captor firmly holding his left arm, he concluded he wasn't dead. Then he noticed the lapels on the German's tunic bore the dreaded "SS" markings and a skull and crossbones insignia was painted on the side of his helmet. The German was sporting two medals on his tunic so Gene knew this guy was a veteran and most definitely was not an old man or a boy. It then dawned on him his own patrol was not to take any prisoners so he assumed the Germans were operating under a similar mandate and began thinking this might be the end of the line for him. He didn't want to let his captor think he was scared, though he was, and the fact he was genuinely having difficulty maintaining his balance helped him disguise his fear.

Soon he was surrounded by a squad of "SS." Their sergeant assigned two of the men to escort Gene and pointed the three of them in the direction of the road bridge. As they began walking, at the best pace Gene could manage, he concluded they were probably going to execute him. Gene still had a phosphorous grenade in his right pants pocket, so when the time came he figured he wouldn't be dying alone as he intended to use it.

They were only about 20 yards up the road when a German soldier appeared out of the dark, walking very deliberately toward Gene and pointing his rifle in a distinctly ominous manner. He came right up to him and pressed the rifle into the center of Gene's forehead, while shouting what Gene figured were probably obscenities. He could see the rifling inside the barrel as the upset soldier brought the gun to his head. He had never been so afraid in his life.

The two guards took a few steps back, deferring to the fact the screaming German was a corporal. Gene wondered if he would have enough time to lower his hands, which were half-raised in the air, yank out the grenade, and take some Germans with him, when he came to the sobering realization: "Well, this is where it ends; I'm not going home."

Just as Gene was about to try to slip his right hand into his pocket to retrieve the grenade, he heard a voice shouting in German, out of the darkness ahead. He glanced up the road and spotted a German officer leading a group of about 30 soldiers. They were quickly running toward him. The out-of-control "SS" corporal didn't lower his gun. It was as if, in his anger, he didn't hear the officer shouting at him as he continued screaming uncontrollably at Gene while keeping his rifle pointed at his forehead.

The officer, an "SS" colonel, ran up to the corporal, paused a moment as he gave Gene a brief once-over, and proceeded to violently swat the rifle right out of the corporal's arms. The corporal was taken by complete surprise as the look on his face changed from outrage to fear when he realized he was facing a colonel. The colonel immediately unleashed a loud and dramatic verbal tirade upon him, thoroughly humbling the would-be executioner.

In a strange way Gene felt some pity for the man, as he'd been the recipient of numerous such tongue-lashings himself. Gene also assumed he and his patrol had just killed a number of the corporal's comrades so he understood his anger. In response to the colonel's lecture the corporal lowered his eyes and mumbled a few words, finishing with "*Ja, meine Standartenführer.*"

The term "führer" caught Gene's attention, as he momentarily considered whether the officer might be Adolf Hitler in the flesh. He stared at the officer, but it wasn't Hitler. Gene's situation had improved, but with so many "SS" around him it was his opinion all the officer had done was to buy him a little time. Nobody gave him a body search so he retained his grenade, intending to use it when the end was imminent.

About four "SS" soldiers quickly surrounded him, one of whom offered Gene a cigarette. Gene, though not a smoker, accepted it, using the only German word he knew: "*Danke.*" Smiling, the German pulled out his lighter, the skull and crossbones insignia of the "SS" emblazoned on its side, and lit the cigarette. Gene discovered it did ease some of the queasiness which had been dogging him since he regained consciousness. Soon about eight more "SS" soldiers appeared out of the darkness and surrounded Gene, looking him over as if he were an interesting exhibit.

One of them removed his helmet and stood next to Gene to point out how Gene, at 6 foot 4 inches tall, towered over the German. One of his comrades made a comment in response, to which they all began laughing. It was about then Gene started to consider the possibility they weren't going to execute him after all and allowed himself to relax a little.

The "SS" men engaged in a conversation with him through a combination of broken English and sign language, as if they were all friends who just happened to be wearing different uniforms than his. One of the Germans tried to explain they didn't understand why the Americans were fighting them when they should be fighting together. He made it clear the Americans and British should be fighting their real enemy, namely, the Communist Russians. Gene realized they were apparently unaware Germany had declared war against the United States, not the other way around. Given the circumstances he didn't attempt to offer an explanation. He was experiencing an incredible headache and was still queasy. Engaging in a sign language-enriched discussion with some "SS" men was just about the last thing he wanted to be doing.

In the interim the colonel had been conferring with another officer. Gene was taken aback when he abruptly turned, pointed to him, and said in very good English: "This way, paratrooper!"

"Yes Sir" was Gene's instinctive response. His feet were still unsteady, but at least the dizziness had let up enough for him to walk without assistance as long as it was at a slow pace.

After a brief pause, while the four "SS" German escorts conferred among themselves, they proceeded up the road in the direction of the objective of Gene's patrol, the road bridge over the River Waal. Gene never anticipated reaching the bridge as a prisoner.

As they began making their way to the rear Gene observed a German "88" and a machine gun were dug in on the hill commanding all the approaches into the Plein. A little further ahead a quadruple antiaircraft gun was mounted on a truck parked beneath the protective canopy of a tree, camouflaged to appear to be nothing other than a large bush.

He observed a squad of German *Fallschirmjäger*, paratroopers, taking up defensive positions. Unfortunately, the vast majority of the Germans he saw were veterans. Eventually he witnessed the sort of soldiers the British and his own general had led him to believe composed their opposition; a mixed platoon of very youthful as well as elderly soldiers.

He wondered what became of the two flanking patrols and if they also found themselves up against an "SS" combat group. It would be many decades before he would learn that Lieutenant Foley's patrol, catching up with his own patrol from the east, had arrived just in time to engage the German troop transports and that bazooka fire was responsible for the massive explosion at the moment he pulled the trigger of his rifle.

Gene was actually lucky to have been captured by the 10th SS Panzer Division "Frundsberg." It would come to be known as the only "SS" division that didn't commit atrocities and would be recognized as having fought a "clean" fight, unlike the balance of the "SS" divisions in World War II. They didn't shoot their prisoners or, for that matter, civilians. Being captured by them was actually a stroke of good fortune; he would live to see another day.

CHAPTER TWELVE

Dinner with "Herr Reichsführer"

After a few minutes the silhouette of an ancient castle began to take shape from out of the dark. To Gene it looked like a square-shaped building on one side with a tower attached to it and pretty much built into the bank of the River Waal. Anyone posted in the tower would have had a commanding view of the entire area, making it a potentially critical defensive outpost. He would later learn the castle was named The Belvedere.

The road bridge over the River Waal was nearby. Despite the loud ringing in his right ear, Gene could clearly discern the racket of heavy vehicular traffic crossing the bridge and coming his way. He realized they never stood a chance to take the bridge. Gene briefly speculated how matters would have developed had they stuck to the original plan to leave the drop zone immediately, locate the river, follow the riverbank to the bridge, and ascertain the situation. He considered the possibility the bridge may have been relatively unguarded had they simply stuck to the original plan. He thought to himself: "What's done is done and nothing's going to change it now."

Mulling over what might have been was not, and still isn't, one of Gene's characteristics. To this day he continues to harbor the belief that had Colonel Lindquist not delayed the patrol by more than four hours they might have discovered a relatively unguarded road bridge. He does, however, question whether they could have held the bridge until relieved.

As they approached the entrance to the castle, "SS" guards stood on either side of the door. He thought it odd that the entry into such an impressive building was so ordinary in size, much like walking into a

After the war Belvedere Castle, in the background, was repurposed into a fine dining restaurant and the interrogation room was converted into storage space.

person's home. Gene noticed the guards wore bands on their arms which appeared to read "Reichsführer SS."

From seemingly out of the clear, images of disappointed Dutch villagers flashed across his mind, for he had no doubt the "SS" had, by then, moved into the enclave Gene had passed through earlier. He was only vaguely aware of the echoes of distant gunfire and again wondered what fate had befallen his patrol.

Gene shook it off as his escorts directed him into the castle and toward a wide, concrete, spiral staircase covered in thick, red velvet carpet. It twisted its way deep into the recesses below. The lighting was barely adequate, which increased the aura of foreboding doom Gene was experiencing. As he was escorted into the bowels of the castle he thought: "Even Hollywood couldn't have dreamt this up."

About every 14 steps they encountered two Schmeisser machine-pistol-armed "SS" guards, one on either side of the stairway. At one point they stopped and allowed a pair of "SS" officers on their way up the stairs to pass them. Gene noticed they were smoking cigarettes, their conversation was argumentative, and they appeared to be in a hurry.

The 14-step pattern continued until they reached the bottom of the stairwell, where he was confronted by two more "SS" guards, one on either side of a large door. Each guard was hugging a machine gun to his chest and they boasted decorations on their perfectly tailored, clean black blouses. The "SS" guards appeared to Gene to be very hardcore as their facial expressions looked as if they'd been carved out of granite.

One of the black-uniformed "SS" guards lightly knocked on the door. When a faint voice came from inside he slipped into the room and quietly closed the door behind him. A few moments later he reappeared and escorted Gene into the room, again gently closing the door behind him as if he were in a church.

When Gene entered the spacious room, he was joined by a pair of machine-gun-toting "SS" men who took up positions on either side of him. As the door closed he felt the guards press a little closer to him, as if they feared he might wander away.

The room was a large rectangle and softly lighted. Ornately framed paintings hung on the walls and the floor was covered in the same thick, red shag carpeting as the stairs. Pairs of additional "SS" guards stood in each of the corners. In the center of the room was an oversized table with a large map spread across it. There were no other furnishings in the room.

Behind the table sat two "SS" officers dressed in what Gene considered to be "pretty nifty" black uniforms. He concluded the officer sitting to his right possessed the air of being in charge. A third "SS" officer was bending down, cap under his left arm, quietly speaking to him. The officer to Gene's left didn't wear either a cap or eyeglasses, was smoking a cigarette, and appeared to be only half-interested in the conversation. Gene assumed the black cap sitting on the table belonged to him.

The discussion sounded to Gene as if the reporting officer was anxious, while the officer he assumed to be their commanding officer listened intently without any display of emotion. When he finished reporting, the officer in charge calmly gave him a series of orders. In response, he abruptly stood at attention, raised his right arm in the Nazi salute, and in a firm voice said: "Heil Hitler!" He quickly made his way out of the room, lighting a cigarette in the process. Another "SS" officer, who had been standing off to the side, immediately walked directly to the same officer and began speaking to him.

Gene figured he must be facing some manner of ad-hoc court martial/ interrogation. He considered himself to be the least-informed paratrooper in all of *Market Garden*, having been pulled from his hospital assignment without the benefit of full mission briefings. Even if he was disposed to giving them any information, there was precious little he could offer, and what he did know, he intended to keep to himself. For the time being, he stood still, the ringing in his ear growing louder in direct proportion to the increased silence.

After a little time passed a light haze of cigarette smoke began to form throughout the room. The "SS" guard to his left nudged Gene with the butt of his machine gun and whispered: *"Das ist Herr Reichsführer!"* Gene had no idea what he meant so he shrugged his shoulders and smiled at him.

Appearing annoyed at Gene's response, the guard again nudged him, a little harder, and whispered: *"Das ist Herr Himmler!"* Using the stock of his machine gun he pointed toward the "SS" officer sitting behind the table, the man Gene had assumed was in charge. Now *that* was a name he recognized. Gene took a good look at the officer the guard had pointed out who, at the moment, was still engaged in conversation with the "SS" officer standing beside him.

At first glance Gene appreciated the fact he strongly resembled Heinrich Himmler. He noted that the man sported a small black moustache, wore round, armless eyeglasses perched on his nose, and was wearing one heck of a fancy black uniform, including a cap featuring the silver "SS" skull and crossbones insignia. Gene concluded it was definitely Herr Himmler. Suddenly he felt very cold. "Holy cow!" he thought to himself: "This can't be good!"

Himmler finished his conversation with the "SS" officer who then quickly exited, causing the guards to push Gene out of the way in the process. Himmler turned to face the officer seated to his right, Gene's left. After a couple of minutes of conversing and referencing the map spread before them he turned his attention to Gene, who, but for the lack of a helmet, would have been nearly the same height as the guards pressing against him. He spent a few moments assessing Gene's appearance, ratcheting up Gene's anxiety all the more.

Himmler may have thought Gene to be "SS" material and possibly considered it a shame he was on the wrong side of the conflict, for Gene was tall, relatively fair-haired and in extremely good physical condition, all the virtues extolled by Himmler. Himmler, for his part, lacked each of those characteristics and his eyes appeared to Gene to be black and cold, very cold. Gene felt a tingling work its way up his spine as he returned Himmler's curious stare.

Through his interpreter, which turned out to be the role of the officer sitting to Himmler's right, Himmler ordered Gene to come forward and stand in front of the table where they were sitting. Gene recognized the over-sized map spread across the table as being a map of Holland. There were large red circles painted around each of Eindhoven, Nijmegen, and Arnhem. Gene felt sick to his stomach at the thought of his comrades walking straight into a prepared German defense. The interrogation commenced.

Himmler would pose a question to the interpreter, who, in turn and in excellent English, would query Gene.

"What's your name, paratrooper?" the interpreter calmly asked.

"Private Eugene Metcalfe, Sir," Gene replied.

"How many men dropped with you today Gene?" The interpreter's demeanor was relaxed, yet somewhat detached, almost as if he were not interested in the answer. He continued: "Excuse me, but do you mind if I call you Gene?" The interpreter smiled as Gene figured he was trying to get friendly by being on a first-name basis, conceivably in the expectation Gene might let his guard down.

Gene thought about it for a moment before answering.

"No Sir, I don't mind if you call me Gene. To answer your question, I'd say there was a ton of us dropped in today."

Gene was under the impression he was probably going to die soon so he figured he had little to lose by giving a "smart-ass answer." There was also no way he could have known that in the week or two prior to *Market Garden* Himmler had transferred an entire combat group of the 16th Panzergrenadier Division of the "Reichsführer SS" from northern Italy to Nijmegen. It was possible the guards on either side of him had taken part in the cold-blooded murder of every man, woman, child, and infant in the town of Sant'Anna di Stazzema, Tuscany, Italy, the month prior. Gene's belief in his imminent demise was valid.

The interpreter appeared confused at Gene's answer. When he conveyed the answer to Himmler, he also seemed puzzled. They proceeded to engage in a short discussion when they were interrupted by a gentle knock on the door. Himmler barked an order in response and an "SS" officer entered the room. In fact he would soon prove to be the first of a nearly constant stream of officers coming and going during the interrogation, most of whom were smoking.

The routine was the same each time an officer entered the room. He would remove his cap and quickly walk over to Himmler, whisper in his ear, wait for a response, and exit. Most of them didn't take the time to perform the "Heil Hitler" salute when leaving. They appeared to Gene as if they were, in his words, "in a hell of a hurry." The continued interruptions proved to significantly slow the interrogation process. Following each interruption the interpreter would pick up precisely where he left off.

"Gene, where was your base?" The interpreter's demeanor struck Gene as almost nonchalant.

Several seconds passed before he responded.

"Sir, it wasn't here, I can tell you that much. You need to understand, Sir, I spent the last 10 or so days in the hospital. My sergeant pulled me out of there and next thing I knew I was in Holland. I missed all the briefings. I'm lucky to even know I'm in Holland."

The questions continued, regardless. All the while "SS" officers were coming and going.

"How was General Gavin this morning?"

Gene smiled broadly as he replied: "Well Sir, Jim appeared to be in good spirits. I'll be sure to let him know of your concerns for his health next time I see him."

Himmler didn't flinch nor did he change his expression each time the interpreter conveyed Gene's responses. Another question was posed.

"What about Colonel Lindquist? Did he make the trip with you?" Gene was quick to reply.

"Sorry Sir. I'm just a private and don't travel in those circles so I really wouldn't know."

Again they conferred.

"And Colonel Warren? Perhaps he was in your plane?"

"No Sir. There were no colonels in my plane."

The interrogation dragged on, interrupted every few minutes by "SS" officers bringing reports to Himmler. As time passed Gene picked up on a mounting atmosphere of urgency in the room. Himmler began asking the "SS" officers more questions than he had earlier and sometimes appeared annoyed with the responses. Never flustered, the interrogator resumed each time.

"Tell me, how was Lieutenant Weaver last time you saw him?" The interpreter paced his questions and was always calm and friendly but Gene wasn't buying it, though the mention of his lieutenant by name was more than a little unsettling. He considered the possibility Weaver had been captured and had already been interrogated.

Another question: "What was your platoon's objective?"

"Sir, I have to assume you know the answer to that one."

It was about then Gene got the feeling they knew a heck of a lot more than he would likely ever know concerning the operation. As far as he could ascertain his entire patrol may have been captured. Nevertheless, the questions continued.

"Look at this map please." The interpreter pointed to an area of the map marked "Groesbeek Heights." Gene edged a little closer, examined the map, and noticed it was an English map. The printing was not in Dutch or German; it was in English. He suddenly felt a little queasy and couldn't be sure whether it was due to his injury or finding himself looking at what appeared to be a good German interpretation of the Allied operations.

"Did you drop at this location today?" The interpreter's tone was nonchalant, as if he already knew the answer.

"Sir, I didn't have a map up on the plane so I really don't know if that's where I dropped in. Again Sir, I missed all the briefings because I was in the hospital for over a week."

Himmler and the interpreter again confided with one another and the questions resumed.

"You say you were in the hospital. What was the reason?"

"Sir, I injured my knee," Gene replied as he pointed to his right leg.

"Of course, I see. So you were discharged from the hospital and sent here?"

"No Sir, I wasn't discharged. My sergeant pulled me out on his own doing so I'm probably listed as AWOL."

As the interpreter translated for Himmler he stumbled over the term "AWOL." The two Germans went back and forth a bit discussing the term when the interpreter returned his attention to Gene.

"This 'AWOL' you mention, what does it mean?" The interpreter actually sounded as if he was intrigued over the term.

"Sir, that's army lingo for 'absent without leave.'"

"Ah, I see," he responded, then conferred with Himmler who shook his head in understanding and even appeared to break a very slight grin.

Gene noticed the grin and got the chills. If ever he had seen pure evil, this man was certainly it. He recognized the fact he was feeling quite intimidated, though no threats had been leveled at him. He recalled feeling intimidated by his former teacher Mr. Hoppe and decided Hoppe couldn't hold a candle to Himmler in, what he referred to as, the "intimidation department."

Himmler and the interpreter consulted yet again.

For at least another half an hour Himmler, through his interpreter, mostly re-hashed earlier questions, occasionally trying to catch Gene off guard in between the constant flow of officers coming and going. Himmler seemed particularly focused on how many men had dropped at Nijmegen, as the interpreter asked the question, using different wording, numerous times. Then the interpreter asked a question he could safely answer:

"Do you have anything in your pockets?"

Gene started to shrug his shoulders, indicating he had nothing with him when he realized he still had a phosphorous grenade in his right-pants pocket.

"Well Sir, I do have a phosphorous grenade your boys missed." Gene's face was without expression, though both the interpreter and Himmler perked up when they heard the response. Based upon Himmler's body language Gene figured Himmler had at least a little knowledge of English. For the first time the interpreter's voice had a bit of urgency to it.

"Put it on the table, right here." He pointed to the center of the map laid out before him.

Gene started to pull out the grenade when he realized the "SS" guards had not been privy to the conversation and might overreact when Gene offered the grenade to Himmler.

"Sir, do those guards know I'm about to produce a grenade?" Gene glanced at the guards as he spoke.

The expression on their faces conveyed to Gene the fact they had not foreseen a potential disaster. If Gene had pulled out a grenade, the guards may well have opened fire with potentially catastrophic results. Himmler, without waiting for the interpretation, immediately spoke to the guards. The interpreter returned to his earlier calm demeanor and said: "It is safe to put it on the table now."

Gene slowly removed the grenade from his pocket and set it on the table; the interpreter grabbed it and handed the grenade over to a guard. There was a short conference and another question was posed.

"Did you have dinner yet?"

He smiled as he was not expecting such a personal question. "No Sir, I've been kinda busy and completely forgot all about it."

"I see," replied the interpreter. He translated Gene's answer which produced a cold half-grin from Himmler. Himmler then abruptly stood and barked orders to the guards at the door. One of them immediately exited the room.

After another brief conference the interpreter simply said: "Thank you, Gene." He then directed him to take a seat on the thickly carpeted floor a few feet to Gene's right, which he did. From his new position he could clearly see Himmler, the interrogator, and the faces of the officers coming in to confer with Himmler. He had no idea what was going to happen next. All he could do was wait and deal with his headache.

About half an hour later the door opened and an "SS" guard carrying a large tray returned. He placed the tray on the carpet in front of Gene and resumed his position guarding the doorway. Gene, a puzzled look on his face, looked over at Himmler. The interpreter said: "For you."

Gene discovered a gallon tin filled with four or five plump, cooked, polish sausages drowning in a dark-colored mustard, a large loaf of a hearty, brown bread and a jar of Belgian orange marmalade. Gene couldn't have been more shocked. He quickly discovered the sausages were, in his words, "really tasty," the mustard "was spicy," and the marmalade "absolutely wonderful."

No doubt Himmler was pleased, as he would occasionally take note of Gene's progress as he continued his map studies and deal with the

The Reichsführer, Heinrich Himmler, sporting his favorite "pince-nez" eyeglasses. Himmler was "given" Holland and Norway as a gift from Adolf Hitler following the "Blitzkrieg" war in the West, June 1940.

continuous flow of officers. For the first time since he awoke to a rifle in his stomach Gene felt reasonably certain he wasn't going to be executed. Little did he know that because of what he would experience over the following eight months it would be almost two years before he could again eat so much food in one sitting.

Shortly after finishing his "dinner," two guards led Gene to a small room with stone walls and a single small window. There were some rudimentary furnishings and an overhead lightbulb. He sat down and contemplated his unfortunate situation. At some point he fell asleep, though not for long.

CHAPTER THIRTEEN

Lent, Holland

At approximately 0300 hours Gene was directed into the back seat of an open-air staff car where he was joined by a sergeant from another 82nd Airborne company. He was hesitant to get into the car for he knew everyone in the 82nd Airborne would be keen to blow up anything moving. When one of the "SS" guards poked his bayonet into Gene's back, he had no choice but to get into the vehicle where he joined the sergeant in the rear seat. It was the first time in his military life he was happy to be in the company of a sergeant.

The irony of driving to the other side of the river, on the very bridge the Allies intended to capture, was not lost on him as he wondered what was to come. During the crossing he observed scores of snipers climbing the bridge's steel girders. From their lofty perches at least 100 feet above the river they could take advantage of a clear field of fire. They could also serve as spotters and relay Allied troop movement to the German defenders. It was September 18, 1944, day two of Operation *Market Garden* and day one of Gene's captivity.

A few minutes later they were dropped off in the town of Lent, just across the bridge and to the north of Nijmegen. A young, neatly dressed, blonde-haired, slightly short, and slender German corporal was assigned to guard them. Gene sized him up and concluded the corporal didn't appear to be very experienced. The man's uniform was too new, his face didn't have the battle-hardened look of a veteran, and he sported no badges or ribbons on his blouse. He was armed only with a Walther P38 semi-automatic pistol, much less menacing than a machine gun or a Schmeisser.

Gene had never met the sergeant from the 82nd Airborne, and while the corporal chatted with a few "SS" soldiers the sergeant whispered to Gene: "We should take this guy out as soon as they're gone."

Gene countered, also in a whisper and while keeping an eye on the corporal: "We have no escape route, we're on the wrong side of the river, there's hundreds of Germans digging in all around us, and we're out in the open. We'd be a whole lot better off biding our time and waiting for a better opportunity to bug outta here."

If he could have thought of another obvious reason he'd have thrown it out there as he felt the sergeant's idea was suicide. The sergeant hesitated so Gene blurted out a final thought: "If you go, you're goin' alone. You'll be shot for sure. We've got to wait!"

The sergeant took a quick glance around them and reluctantly agreed with Gene.

The corporal, unaware his prisoners had been conversing, bid the two "SS" in the staff car goodbye and motioned for Gene and the sergeant to follow him. He led his two prisoners through an orchard in which hundreds of Germans were digging in for a fight. Their destination proved to be on the far side of the orchard in the form of a square-shaped shed. Upon arriving the corporal opened what proved to be a very squeaky door and indicated for them to follow him inside where all the tools needed to operate an orchard were stored.

There was a small round table in the middle of the room. The corporal dragged it over to the sole window and took up a position sitting on one edge of the table. From there he had a pretty good view of the action taking place throughout the orchard. He pulled a candle from his jacket pocket, positioned it at the center of the table, and proceeded to light it while never letting go of the pistol. Gene and the sergeant made themselves as comfortable as they could. Gene had a bad feeling in his gut about the location the corporal chose and made certain he had at least a partial view through the window so he could monitor what was going on outside. It wasn't the first and wouldn't be the last time his instincts would warn him of danger.

He strained his neck as he peered out the window and noticed the Germans were setting up a pair of "88" artillery emplacements very close to their position. Alarmed, he tried using sign language to convince the corporal this was not a good place to hang out. He knew once they began to fire, Allied spotters would probably notice the muzzle flashes from the "88s." In response the Allies would seek to take out the two artillery pieces along with everything else in the vicinity.

Unfortunately the corporal failed to recognize the danger lurking nearby, so Gene and the sergeant positioned themselves a little closer to the door in the event they needed to get out in a hurry. The only noise penetrating the night air was from the Germans digging their entrenchments; otherwise there was no indication a battle was taking place anywhere near them.

They had been in the shed about half an hour when an Allied artillery barrage began, though the Germans had not yet commenced firing themselves. Gene concluded the artillery must have been brought in by glider earlier in the day and it was now all too apparent they were in the target zone.

With great interest Gene watched as the incoming shells, in clusters of four, rained down upon the orchard. There would be three explosions in a horizontal line, left-to-right, followed by a fourth to the rear and in the center of the first three shell bursts. The next three shells would land closer to their position, followed by a fourth shell landing a bit behind the three.

Gene realized the deadly pattern of artillery fire was coming directly at them and frantically tried to convince the corporal they were about to be bracketed by the incoming barrage when a shell landed just outside the front door. Gene's common sense told him the next round would land on top of them. He suddenly bolted for the door and yelled as loudly as he could: "Outen! I'm getting out!"

Gene, with the sergeant and the German corporal close on his heels, ran like hell and dove into a nearby foxhole where the three men landed on top of several German soldiers. Gene didn't pay any attention to what he termed, "their jabbering." When the soldiers realized the three intruders provided them a little more protection, in the form of their bodies, they quieted down. In a matter of seconds the shed from which they fled suffered a direct hit and completely disintegrated.

The bombardment lasted for what felt to Gene like hours. Eventually the shelling ceased, though only long enough for all of the trench-mates to get a little shut-eye.

In a little while they were awakened by what sounded to Gene like a "boxcar flying overhead." Moments later there was an explosion several miles distant followed by a secondary explosion; the horizon lit up just about where Gene had dropped the day prior. More time passed and everything was dead-silent until a second boxcar-like sound went overhead, resulting in a larger explosion than previous. Gene considered the possibility the shell had struck an ammo dump.

Gene and the sergeant couldn't figure out what the heck kind of cannon the Germans were firing, but they did know the Germans had locked in on their landing zone. By then the area would have been cluttered with scores of gliders and all manner of supplies, including Jeeps, light artillery, ammo, fuel, and men. It wasn't long before the Allies began to return fire. As the Allied artillery began to drop closer and closer the corporal yelled out: "*Folge mir!*"

He stood up and began to run across the orchard toward a house situated on its far end. Gene and the sergeant didn't waste time and quickly joined him. They were running as hard as they could, often stumbling over downed branches and dead bodies in the darkness, explosions throwing up debris all around them.

Gene heard a "zizz" sound coming toward him and yelled: "Oh shit!" All three of them dove head-first into the dirt and put their hands over their heads. In a moment there was an earsplitting explosion and they were immediately showered with mud and tree limbs. As they got up and continued their dash, the incoming artillery barrage proved unrelenting. The blasts churned up the orchard, downing trees and causing havoc. More often than not each shell burst was followed by the screams of the helpless and overly exposed German soldiers. It was a terrifying experience.

They were continuously dodging falling branches and were forced to dive for cover three more times before they finally reached the house, unscathed. They burst into the living room just as a shell landed outside, shattering all the windows and showering glass shards throughout the room. Gene immediately lunged into a very large stone fireplace located on the far wall where he was quickly joined by the sergeant and, lastly, the corporal.

They nestled together in the stone enclosure as the house shook from numerous nearby shell bursts, plaster falling from the ceiling with each explosion. Apparently the Allied spotters weren't able to view the house in the early pre-dawn light or it probably would have been targeted for it was the sole structure remaining in the orchard. The barrage ended as abruptly as it began, the resulting silence broken only by the haunting cries of the wounded soldiers scattered about the orchard.

The lull didn't last long. Soon the German "88s" began returning the fire, the "boom, boom, boom" sound they made being distinctly different from the incoming Allied rounds. It wasn't long before Gene realized the "88s" had been repositioned no more than a hundred feet from the house. They hadn't noticed the cannons due to the darkness, the light fog, and the fact they were running for their lives at the time.

Unfortunately, Allied spotters could easily observe the barrel flashes as the Germans fired. Allied artillery, once again, began to rain down on the orchard. Gene prayed the German gunners would either be quickly annihilated or move the hell out of there. His prayers were answered when he heard the sound of truck engines. He breathed a sigh of relief when he realized the Germans were quickly repositioning their "88s."

With nowhere to run the three men eventually dozed off, huddled within the relatively safe, albeit very sooty, confines of the fireplace. Finally the sun began to rise and the corporal indicated it was time to leave. When he tried to open the door he discovered the sole entry to the house was blocked by a fallen tree limb, forcing them to exit through a blown-out window instead.

A little later in the morning Gene was taken to an aid station and assigned to assist a German medical team, as there were hundreds of wounded and dead Germans scattered throughout the ruined orchard. The corporal, with the sergeant in tow, proceeded to disappear in the opposite direction. He would never see the sergeant again.

The moans and cries of the wounded were difficult for Gene to cope with; for the first time in his life he was surrounded by death and dismemberment. In one instance Gene picked up a young soldier who he believed couldn't have been more than 15 years old. As he gently lifted the boy Gene's right hand sunk deeply into the young man's shrapnel-ripped back. The boy was crying and asking for water. Gene motioned to the attending medic with a canteen and he somberly agreed Gene could let him drink. As Gene gently laid the boy into an ambulance, the ambulance orderly performed a brief examination and indicated he thought the boy was a "goner."

Gene spent a long, emotionally and physically draining day carrying wounded to ambulance vehicles, moving dead Germans to a makeshift open morgue, and occasionally dodging incoming artillery rounds. He considered the probability his fellow paratroopers across the river might never know how devastatingly effective their barrages had been.

At about 1800 hours the corporal returned without the sergeant. He led Gene to the riverbank, where a long, narrow motorboat was waiting to pick them up. The operator of the boat was an older German soldier who appeared to be nervous, as he repeatedly scanned the far bank of the river as if expecting trouble.

In sign language the corporal indicated to Gene he was taking him to the opposite side of the River Waal, meaning he'd be on the same side of the river as the 82nd Airborne. He began thinking of the possibility of slipping away during the night and working his way back to the 508th. Though the motorboat could easily hold more than three men, it was only the corporal, Gene, and the operator making the trip across. Gene believed getting to the other side of the river increased the likelihood he could manage a successful escape. He was excited at the prospect.

As they began the 400-yard crossing of the rapidly flowing river, Gene heard what he described as a "flying boxcar whoosh" screaming overhead, the same unnerving sound he'd heard the night before. At the time he couldn't imagine what manner of gun could possibly fire a shell as large as the one passing overhead must have been. All he knew was it seemed to be coming from pretty far behind the front lines, for he never heard anything resembling a cannon discharge. Later that night he would discover it was actually a shell from a huge, railroad-mounted cannon.

Until then he had not appreciated how wide the river was, let alone how fast it was flowing. It gave him an appreciation for the importance of capturing the road bridge intact, as constructing a pontoon bridge was, in his opinion, next to impossible. In all events, constructing a temporary bridge would require a great deal of precious time and he knew time was of the essence for the Allies.

When the boat reached the midpoint of the river they found themselves surrounded by a series of small explosions. Water spouts as high as about

6 feet were appearing all around the boat and seemed to be originating from somewhere behind them. They didn't resemble artillery or mortar fire because they were striking the water at a nearly 45-degree angle and the water spouts were too small. Gene immediately turned to look behind him and realized the explosions were coming from a pair of Messerschmitt 109 fighter planes firing their cannons at a lone P-51 Mustang.

The three planes, throttles wide open, were diving to a height not more than 30 feet above the river and were rushing at them with their machine guns and cannons blazing away. Gene instinctively ducked as the three planes flew past. The motorman was so scared he fully opened the throttle and made directly for the remnants of a dock adjoining, what Gene recalls, a "postcard perfect" working windmill on the near side of the river, "its long arms turning slowly in a large, diametric circle."

When the motorman reached the dock, he barely slowed down and just scarcely avoided colliding with it, crashing instead into the muddy, sloping river bank. Without stopping to tether the boat he leapt onto the slippery bank and ran toward the windmill. Gene glanced around and, after noting a nearby machine-gun emplacement, decided to follow the fleeing boat operator into the mill. After initially hesitating, the corporal, who had been watching the three planes as they executed a series of hard banks, climbs and dives, also fled for the presumed safety of the windmill.

When Gene entered the structure he noticed the miller was calmly working the grinding apparatus, oblivious to the drama taking place in the sky outside. Gene, the corporal, and the motorman all scrambled to look out the windows.

After a few moments they observed the apparently undamaged P-51 climb to about 500 feet and make a hard bank to the left. The canopy opened and Gene witnessed the pilot safely parachute from the plane. It looked to him as if the pilot would be landing on Gene's side of the river not too far from the mill. He watched the pilot's parachute oscillate a few times, then disappear behind a stand of tall trees. The P-51 was turning end-over-end and crashed into the ground in a twisting motion followed by a loud explosion, a cloud of black smoke and flame marking the crash site. The two Messerschmitt fighters circled several times before speeding away.

With the drama of the one-sided dogfight over, Gene turned his attention to the large room in which he found himself. A few feet away stood the miller, covered in white flour and grinding grain in the traditional method of stone-on-stone, the power supplied by the slowly turning windmill. It was early Monday evening, September 19, 1945. The miller was quietly at work, his only concern being the job at hand.

Gene took a sitting position on the floor, his back to the stone wall, and spent a little time observing the man diligently ply his trade. As he watched the great stone wheel turning, he thought if it weren't for the circumstances this would otherwise be a "wonderful educational treat."

After watching the miller hard at work for about 20 minutes, a pair of what he thought must be mirages walked into the room. He found himself facing two amazingly beautiful girls. They were twins, about 18 years old and cloaked in traditional, intricately detailed dresses. Their blonde hair was pulled back into tight, long braids and trailed behind them.

The girls were smiling and giggling as they alternately glanced at Gene, who had immediately stood and was smiling back at them, while speaking to each other in Dutch. Gene didn't understand the words though he was aware they were talking about the American and he was the only American present. They brought with them bread and soup which the miller shared with Gene and his captor, the motorboat operator having quietly slipped out the door earlier. As he ate the first real food he had sampled since his dinner with Himmler, Gene wondered to himself: "How can life be so wonderful in the ugly stench of war?"

A couple of hours passed and the artillery and small-arms fire had quieted down as twilight was slowly setting in. Suddenly the door burst open and two German Fallschirmjägers escorted a slender-built, Army Air Corps second lieutenant into the room. The young officer was dressed in khakis, including a khaki necktie, and was wearing house slippers and a fancy overseas cap. He sported campaign ribbons on his chest. His face featured a narrow black moustache which overly accentuated his rather round cheeks. He was only about 5 feet 7 inches tall and appeared to be 22 years old. Gene quickly surmised he was the pilot of the crashed P-51.

Never one to concern himself over a person's rank, Gene walked up to the pilot and said: "Why the hell did you bail out of a perfectly good plane?"

"They had me," he meekly replied, his eyes focused on the wood floor rather than on Gene.

"And what are you all dressed up for? Didn't you know you'd be flying a sortie today?" Gene asked.

"I had a date when I got back and figured I wouldn't have time to change," the pilot responded.

Gene, fairly disgusted with the pilot, decided to ignore him. He did, on the other hand, consider the life the pilot had been leading, combat by day and English girls by night, to have been "pretty cozy." About an hour later there was a deafening roar overhead, causing everyone in the mill, except the pilot, to duck. The pilot chuckled as he explained the roar was that of a Messerschmitt 262 jet fighter. To this day each time Gene hears a jet flying overhead he recalls his first experience with the sound of jet engines.

In the early evening a canvas-covered troop truck pulled up to the mill. The corporal, Gene, and the pilot piled into the back and soon were headed toward Germany. They'd only been traveling for a short while when the truck screeched to a sudden stop. The corporal peered out the back as the unmistakable sound of a P-47 Thunderbolt flying directly overhead, just above the treetops, pierced the otherwise quiet surroundings.

The quick-thinking driver had abruptly pulled under the cover of a nearby stand of stately elm trees. Moments later the P-47 returned, flying just above the treetops, apparently searching for Gene's truck. He flew over one more time before disappearing into the distance. After the

A German "Gustav" railway cannon.

near-miss the truck driver changed his mind about daylight travel and waited for darkness to set in before continuing.

It was another instance where, but for chance timing, Gene could have been killed by Allied forces. Had the P-47 arrived one minute earlier, he, more likely than not, would have been able to catch the truck on the open road and blasted it, along with Gene and the P-51 pilot, into oblivion.

Once darkness fully set in the driver resumed the journey. After traveling without respite for several hours, he apparently decided to take a break and stopped in a small town where there was a railhead and several sidings. Plenty of darkness remained and Gene was beginning to wonder how long they'd be stopping when the sky was suddenly set alight by flares from a British night-fighter. The flares perfectly illuminated a huge railway cannon mounted on two flatcars, parked on a siding only a couple hundred feet away from them.

Gene realized "the monster-sized cannon" must have been the source of the boxcar-like "swooshes" he'd heard. The immediate issue was the fact everything surrounding the railway cannon was drenched in artificial daylight, including Gene's truck. The flares offered up easy targets for the fighter which swooped in, guns blazing. However, his machine guns were completely ineffective against the iron monster of a cannon which proved to be his focus. Gene's canvas-covered transport and the nearby boxcars sitting on a siding remained intact.

The fighter made several equally ineffective passes, and just as suddenly as it appeared, it was gone. The truck driver immediately pulled back onto the road and sped away as fast as road conditions allowed. In fact, it was almost a little too fast; as he weaved back and forth across the rutted roadway the vehicle tilted dangerously from one side to the other. Once safely clear of the railway gun, he slowed to a more reasonable pace and Gene stopped worrying about dying in a one-vehicle truck accident.

CHAPTER FOURTEEN

Stalag XII-A

Gene's destination turned out to be Stalag XII-A, in Limburg, Germany. As they approached Limburg he was impressed by the beauty of the picturesque town situated at the base of a large hill. On the crest of the hill sat what, in Gene's opinion, was a very impressive castle. His new surroundings would prove to be a stark contrast to the beauty of the countryside surrounding the Stalag.

By the time he arrived Gene was quite hungry. The Germans had barely fed him since Belvedere Castle. Except for the graciousness of the miller and his twin daughters, he'd have been starved.

As he marched into camp with his fellow prisoners, mostly paratroopers, he realized the Stalag was a remarkable mix of every nationality engaged in the war. He was initially fascinated by Stalag XII-A for its considerable size; the sprawling encampment appeared to go on forever.

The prison camp primarily served as a transitory camp where the Germans processed all new prisoners of war (POWs), without regard as to nationality or where they were captured. Once processed, most of them would be assigned to a permanent Stalag, which would be matched with each prisoner's country of origin, rank, and service branch. Gene grew depressed at the sight of thousands upon thousands of prisoners and wondered whether his impression that the Allies were winning the war was wrong. His initial fascination was quickly disintegrating into the numbness of utter despair.

He didn't notice any wooden barracks or, for that matter, anything resembling furnishings in the American section of the Stalag. Instead, there was a series of very large tents, almost as if a circus were in town.

Entrance to Stalag XII-A following liberation. (Photo courtesy of Mr. and Mrs. Eugene Metcalfe)

The problem for Gene was the clowns were carrying machine guns, and, as he soon learned, they truly enjoyed using them on their audience.

The conditions at XII-A were outrageously bad and life there was both miserable and boring. Within the tents there were no cots, mattresses, pillows, blankets, heat, water or electricity; the floor of the tent was straw-covered dirt, and it was so crowded there was barely room for all of the men to find a place to lie down each night.

The latrines were a source of dysentery and other potentially deadly diseases. Diarrhea and dehydration were rampant. Gene, on the advice of others, minimized his use of the latrines as best he could.

Gene considered the meals to be a cruel joke. They might consist of a small potato, a half slice of dark bread, and sometimes a semi-clear liquid they labeled as "soup." Occasionally the meals might include unidentifiable items Gene was expected to eat; and eat he did, as the alternative was death. Hunger soon became a constant companion along with an ever-present sense of fear for his life.

The morning after his arrival Gene found himself facing an interrogator, except the pudgy German sergeant performing the interrogation was nowhere near as intimidating as Himmler had been. The sergeant casually queried him as to his name and rank. After a few moments' pause he asked what Gene had done for a living before the war. Without thinking, Gene blurted out he had been a farmer. At the time he considered it to be a relatively harmless answer and had no idea it would likely save his life in the not-too-distant future.

Gene quietly chuckled when he heard a paratrooper at the next table reply to the same question: "I was a Burgermeister." "Burgermeister?" replied the incredulous interrogator. "You look too young to have been a Burgermeister." The young paratrooper stuck to his story as the men within hearing range enjoyed a moment of comic relief at the interrogator's expense.

Weeks later he would realize some of the questions presented to him were for the purpose of determining whether he had any Jewish blood in his family history. The questions seemed harmless enough at the time, but as another prisoner eventually pointed out to him the Germans never asked a question that wasn't somehow "loaded."

They took Gene's photograph and issued him German prisoner-of-war dog tags with a new serial number. It was explained to him wearing the dog tags was absolutely mandatory at the cost of being shot should he, or any other prisoner, ever be discovered without them hanging around their respective necks.

The foul air inside of the tent proved to be a strong motivation for him to spend as much time as possible out in the open. There were no activities in which to participate, so he joined his fellow prisoners as they aimlessly strolled around the perimeter of the compound. In a strange way it reminded him of a high school dance.

The Germans made it clear the prisoners were not to venture anywhere near the barbed-wire-encrusted fences. There was a single wire running roughly 10–12 feet parallel to the main fencing all around the camp, about 12 inches off the ground. The area between the short wire and the fence was commonly referred to as "no-man's land." There was a valid reason for the moniker.

It was on one such walk he noticed a passing German guard had tossed a still-burning cigarette into no-man's land. It couldn't have been more than 2 inches long. One of the prisoners started to retrieve it and immediately drew the attention of the guard in a nearby guard tower. The guard shouted at him: "*Verboten! Verboten!*" and "*Nein! Nein!*"

The prisoner, a British paratrooper, stopped, looked up at the guard and pointed in the direction of the still-burning cigarette. With his right hand he made a motion of bringing the cigarette to his lips.

The guard firmly repeated: "*Nein! Nein!*" and aimed his machine gun at him. The soldier apparently thought he was bluffing, ignored him, and stepped over the short wire. Just as he began reaching down to pick up the cigarette the guard machine-gunned him to death. Scores of fellow prisoners witnessed the murder. As Gene stood petrified and in shock, from out of the blue he suddenly recalled Mr. Johnson's advice not to take up smoking for "it could kill you."

Without any type of lighting inside the tents, it was essential Gene find a piece of ground to sleep on before nightfall. If a prisoner waited too long it would be impossible to find a sleeping space in the pitch-dark, over-crowded tent. Without electricity there was nothing for anyone to do after dark except sleep, which thankfully came easily for him. It was the only time Gene could forget where he was.

In his first full day at the Stalag, the camp's air-raid sirens began to sound in the late afternoon. Large formations of American bombers were flying overhead, something the Germans did not desire the prisoners to witness. While there was no real danger of being bombed, it was absolutely mandatory for all of the prisoners to huddle inside their tents, for the failure to do so could be dramatic. The Germans didn't want the prisoners to take heart at the appearance of Allied bomber formations flying unmolested overhead and were determined to enforce their air-raid rules.

Gene was sitting near the entry to his tent, safely inside, watching a fellow prisoner. The prisoner was, at great personal risk, still standing a few yards outside of the tent. He was an American paratrooper and would point at the bombers flying overhead, then point at the guard in the tower and laugh out loud. To further aggravate the guard he feigned he was laughing so hard he had to bend forward to keep from falling.

Suddenly the prisoner stood upright and turned to dash into the tent. But it was too late; the guard in the tower opened fire on him with his machine gun. Three bullets struck the unfortunate man in the back and a fourth lodged in one of his legs. The force of the impacts sent him sprawling directly on top of a startled Gene. At the same moment a bullet intended for the fleeing prisoner whizzed past his left ear, missing him by less than an inch. To this day Gene recalls how close to being shot in the head he had come.

Gene didn't hesitate as he immediately stood and picked up the heavily bleeding and unconscious man—a man he didn't even know. He looked around at his fellow prisoners standing nearby, all of whom were silently watching him.

"Anyone going to help? I'm taking him over to the hospital tent." Gene looked around to discover there were no takers. In fact, everyone was trying to look anywhere except at Gene as the air-raid sirens continued to blare.

"Well, I can't just leave him here to die. Wish me luck!" Gene exclaimed.

Heaving the bleeding man over his shoulder, he stepped out of the tent where three guards standing outside of the fence were aiming their rifles directly at his head, vigorously indicating he needed to turn around. He glanced up at the guard tower and was confronted by the same machine-gunner who had just shot up the profusely bleeding man in his arms. He knew he was in imminent danger of suffering the same fate.

He had to make a quick decision. Gene looked around and noticed a couple of the guards pointing their rifles at his head were wearing medals from the Winter War. He concluded the medals indicated they were veterans and had probably carried off their own wounded at one time or another, just as he was trying to do. He knew time was of the essence and took a chance.

Gene pointed to the Red Cross painted on the roof of the hospital, about 150 feet away, as he attempted to convey to the guards his intention to carry the wounded man there. They didn't lower their rifles. As he took a short, somewhat hesitant first step, they didn't fire. Nor did they try to force him back into the tent. Instead, they continued to menacingly point their guns at him.

They didn't appear as if they truly intended to shoot him so he took a chance—a big chance, for he was about to intentionally put himself into harm's way. He was aware there were only two possible outcomes to his action and chose not to consider the more permanent of the two.

Slowly, one little step at a time, he made the perilous trek to the hospital tent where a British doctor, apparently having witnessed the shooting, was waiting for him. Gene delivered the wounded man into his care and waited for the "all-clear" siren, at which time he returned to his tent without further incident. The front of his battle jacket and trousers were drenched in blood, clothing he would wear for eight more months. With no access to water and soap there was nothing he could do about it.

Fifty-two years later, while on a vacation in Colorado, Gene would receive a phone call from Elmer Melchi, explaining he was the man Gene had carried to the hospital tent at Stalag XII-A. It was not until then that Gene would know the man he risked his life for had survived. It was one of many amazing postwar reunions Gene would experience.

CHAPTER FIFTEEN

Five Days in Hell

Following a relatively short stay in Stalag XII-A, Gene, about a dozen fellow paratroopers, and hundreds of other Allied prisoners of war found themselves in a railroad marshalling yard where they were to board a train bound for their next Stalag. A few hundred feet away a group of approximately 300 American and British officers were in the process of loading onto a long string of boxcars when suddenly the roar of planes flying overhead sent everyone scurrying in search of cover. For the 300 officers it was too late, as the bombs fell directly into their midst, killing most, if not all, of them. Again, somehow, Gene managed to just miss death from friendly fire.

Once the coast was clear, Gene and his fellow paratroopers were herded into a long trainload of fellow prisoners of war. The paratroopers on the train were eventually disembarked at Luftwaffe prisoner-of-war camp Stalag Luft III. Gene had no way of knowing the Luftwaffe camp would one day prove the basis for the movie *The Great Escape*. What he did know was the Luftwaffe treated them much better than they had been treated at Stalag XII-A.

At Luft III they joined with other recently arrived paratroopers, bringing their ranks up to about several dozen in total. They were provided with wooden bunkhouses featuring electricity, water, heat, bunkbeds, showers, and better, albeit still bad, food. There was even a genuine hospital on the grounds. A veteran of the Stalag told Gene he could expect to receive a Red Cross package each week containing food and other essential items to make life a little more bearable.

Unfortunately, he would not be there long enough to determine the veracity of the claim.

It was Gene's understanding that in the German manner of thinking German paratroopers were part of the Luftwaffe, for without planes they couldn't be paratroopers. The Germans applied the same logic to the American paratroopers, resulting in Gene and his fellow paratrooper/prisoners becoming guests of the Luftwaffe. To its credit the Luftwaffe exhibited something of a fondness for members of the opposing air forces, including paratroopers; thus conditions were always better at one of their Stalags than at a typical prisoner-of war camp.

Gene had not been there a day when word began spreading amongst the paratroopers that their senior officer at the Stalag, Army Air Force Colonel Delmar Spivey, was making a big stink with the camp's commandant. Apparently Spivey was very upset over the fact paratroopers were being barracked in a Luftwaffe camp. The colonel was demanding they be sent to a camp with other infantrymen, not to be confused with Army Air Force personnel.

Following two or three days of absolute hell-raising with the camp commandant, Gene and roughly 80 other paratroopers were marched to a railroad yard where they were forced into World War I era boxcars with a few hundred additional American and British prisoners, 40–50 men in each car. They were not cattle cars with open slots to let in fresh air; they were more like rolling wooden caskets and notably smaller than the average boxcar of the day. The only penetrating light within the cramped confines was from holes in the wooden walls where there had been bomb damage. There was no water. There was no food. There was no latrine. Gene and a couple of others took it upon themselves to designate one small corner of the boxcar to function as a latrine. It wasn't long before a truly foul odor permeated every inch of space, further increasing the level of misery and despair.

Trains seldom moved during daylight due to the danger of being attacked by Allied warplanes. In addition, the Germans didn't mark POW trains with any identifying markings or insignias a pilot might recognize, so their train would appear to be as any other train, a legitimate military target even if they were parked on a siding.

Sitting on railroad sidings all day was nerve-wracking, not knowing whether a fighter pilot might decide to attack them, as the boxcars certainly appeared to be military targets. Prior to boarding they had been told München (Munich) was their destination, which should have been a fairly easy and relatively short trip. Unfortunately, the Germans apparently considered POW trains to be last on the German High Command totem pole of shipping priorities. When his train moved it was only for a couple of hours at a time and always under cover of darkness.

Gene and his fellow prisoners had no way of knowing they would spend the next five days and nights locked inside the boxcar without water or food. On the second day it became obvious the Germans did not intend to provide them with food, let alone any water and they decided they'd better hydrate the best way they could. On the second night they were parked at a siding when the British bombed the railyard. Bomb fragments pierced the wooden walls of the freight car and, at one point, the concussion of an exploding bomb tilted the entire car almost to the point of rolling onto its side. Again Gene had barely escaped death, or severe injury, at the hands of the Allies.

As they sat idle on various railroad sidings he could hear railroad traffic rushing past them while they stagnated in the filth and darkness. After three days some of the sick and wounded men began to die. The survivors carefully stacked the deceased in the corner of the boxcar across from the latrine. By the fifth day there was literally a pile of dead bodies. Gene wondered how many more paratroopers died, not to mention the hundreds of other prisoners who were on that railroad journey through hell.

Sometime during the fifth night the train stopped after only a brief period of travel. The Germans opened the doors and demanded they exit. All of the men, Gene included, were too weak and stiff to stand. Before exiting they were ordered to heave the bodies of the dead out of the car first.

Gene found it necessary to roll his severely dehydrated and malnourished body out of the car. He then tumbled several feet to the ground, where he and his fellow survivors landed on their deceased companions, softening the otherwise hard landing. Once on the ground it was necessary they help each other stand upright. They were immediately force-marched a mile to their new camp, four abreast. Guard dogs nipped at them while the German guards struck the slower-moving prisoners with their rifle butts.

Gene looked around and calculated there appeared to be about 30 percent fewer men than were present on the march to the train five days earlier. From his position he was not able to observe whether Colonel Spivey was among them and for the colonel's sake it was probably a good thing. What Gene and his fellow paratroopers didn't know was the colonel was safe, back at Stalag Luft III, and would remain a "guest" of the Luftwaffe until liberation. Whether he ever learned the fate of the paratroopers he caused to be expelled from the Luft camp is something Gene would never be able to determine.

CHAPTER SIXTEEN

Stalag VII-A

The bucolic sight of acre upon acre of potato fields dotted by occasional stands of trees did not prepare Gene for what he was about to confront. As he rounded the street corner alongside an old cheese factory, he came face-to-face with the camp for the first time. Chills ran up and down his spine at the spectacle of very tall barbed-wire fencing announcing the Stalag's presence.

Stalag VII-A would be Gene's new home. It was located adjacent to the small town of Moosburg, Germany, near the Austrian border and a relatively quick train ride from München. At the time of Gene's arrival Stalag VII-A was home to about 110,000 prisoners of war representing every front in which Germany had been engaged. Within the sprawling network of structures the prisoners were segregated into separate compounds based first on country of origin and further segregated based on rank. The various compounds were cordoned off from one another by barbed-wire fencing.

The barbed-wire barriers were further reinforced with guard towers, each manned by guards who, Gene thought, looked as if they were guarding the gates of hell. Some of the soldiers manning the towers carried rifles, while others held machine guns across their torsos. All of the tower guards were intently monitoring the incoming procession of new prisoners.

The smoking cigarette incident at Stalag XII-A came rushing from his memory, causing Gene to consider whether the guards were hoping for an opportunity to conduct a little bit of live target practice. Events would soon prove there was a legitimate foundation for his anxiety.

As he passed through the main gate he noticed the barbed-wire fences utilized the same 10–12-foot-wide no-man's land as had been present at the prior two camps. He assumed the Germans insisted there always be a clear expanse of vacant space on the interior side of the fencing and certainly appeared to be consistent in their application of the rule.

Numerous French soldiers were milling about their compound, which was on one side of the American compound, while the Russians were on the other side. The British compound, he would later learn, was on the far side of the French barracks. About a dozen curious Frenchmen were looking over the newly arriving Americans when one of them noticed someone had tossed a still-burning cigarette into no-man's land. For Gene, it was about to be a case of déjà vu.

One unfortunate Frenchman couldn't resist the temptation, possibly because he had simply had enough with life. His dark eyes were sunken into his skull, exaggerating the effect of the heavy, purple bags of skin hanging below them. His unshaven cheeks were nothing more than skin pulled against bone, and his worn-out uniform appeared to be several sizes too large. The man had wrapped cloth around his feet in what looked to be an effort to prevent his boots from completely falling apart.

He was staring at the burning cigarette when suddenly he stepped over the low wire to retrieve it. The tower guard vehemently yelled at him: "*Nein! Nein! Verboten!*" Apparently oblivious to the warning, he paid no attention to the threat and continued. As he began to bend over and reach for the smoking cigarette, the guard fired. His shot struck him in the side of the head, blowing off his knit cap and killing him instantly. He had broken a cardinal rule: under no circumstances can a prisoner cross the 12-inch-tall wire demarking no-man's land.

Before Gene even had a chance to settle into his new surroundings he found himself further shaken by the almost ghost-like appearance of his fellow prisoners; they were little more than walking skeletons. He became nauseous and nearly vomited when he grasped the realization he was destined to a similar fate. Someone pointed him to his bunk, where he sat down and briefly closed his eyes until he regained control of himself.

Gene thought it ironic the nickname of his high school team was the "Barbs," given he was confined by miles of barbed wire. His hometown of DeKalb happened to be where barbed wire was invented, thus the nickname. Since his capture barbed wire had taken on an entirely different meaning and he vowed, should he survive the war, never to use the stuff.

After only one day in Stalag VII-A he concluded the Luftwaffe appeared to have been running a country club at Stalag Luft III when compared to the conditions he faced at VII-A. Images of Colonel Spivey complaining to the Stalag's commandant still floated in his head, along with the truly hellish and deadly train ride to Moosburg. His stomach was still in full revolt, having been denied food and water for five days. Finding no relief for his hunger, he tried to compensate with water.

Though only a prisoner for fewer than two weeks he had come to understand his German captors were true masters of knowing just how little food was needed to keep a man alive. He felt the Wehrmacht and "SS" martinets running Stalag VII-A had elevated starvation to the status of an art form. He quickly learned to eat as slowly as possible in an attempt to trick his brain into thinking he was eating more than he was. The trick didn't work. He continued the practice regardless.

The living conditions at VII-A made the spread of disease and death an ever-present reality for the severely undernourished population. Each of the barracks had been designed to house 150 prisoners. In reality, there were at least 300 prisoners in his barracks and exactly one water spigot.

The fact water service was intermittently cut off, sometimes due to errant Allied bombing and other times for no explanation at all, made keeping himself relatively clean nearly impossible, especially as the cold weather set in. The Germans lacked an incentive to provide better food, water service or latrines as, in Gene's opinion, they appeared to consider themselves better off each time a prisoner died for the pragmatic reason each death made their lives easier.

Breakfast consisted of a little bit of foul-tasting tea and a half-slice of black bread. Lunch was provided only to prisoners out on a slave/work detail in München. Lunch was not part of the camp's culinary itinerary.

Dinner at Stalag VII-A was something Gene considered to be truly disgusting. It consisted of a pale green soup, the flavor of which Gene had

A funeral procession at Stalag VII-A. As a general rule when a prisoner died his body was placed in either a wheelbarrow or a two-wheeled cart and buried without a casket. The men in the caskets shown above apparently were particularly beloved.

never experienced and to this day cannot find the words to adequately convey how repulsive it was. Sometimes he might discover a bit of a potato or perhaps a turnip-top to accompany the soup. Either a half-slice or sometimes a whole slice of the same black bread served at breakfast would supplement dinner. It was not long before he was pulling his belt so tightly around his shrinking waist it became necessary to fold the excess leather back under itself to keep it from flapping.

From what he could observe of the other compounds, be they English, French or Russian, they all seemed to be faring at least as poorly as his own compound. There was a notable exception: the Sikhs.

The Sikhs wore immaculate white uniforms with sparkling white turbans. They conducted organized calisthenics and spent the afternoons practicing military drills. The Sikhs also prepared their own food, as the Germans appeared to make concessions to their religious beliefs and would leave sacks of grain at their compound entrance. The Germans did not serve any food to the Sikhs as the Sikhs controlled their own food and utensil storage, food preparation, and the related clean-up and waste disposal. Gene considered them to be very disciplined and thought the Germans might harbor an appreciation for their practices. In any event, it was difficult for him to believe they were part of the same Stalag.

He was at the camp for just under two weeks when he experienced what the American Red Cross intended to be the weekly distribution of a Red Cross parcel, only to learn each parcel had to be shared equally by 20 men. He had been told by a fellow prisoner at Stalag Luft III that each man received his own Red Cross parcel, but somehow Stalag VII-A was exempt. He had no way of knowing the Germans were storing the other 19 parcels, multiplied by thousands of men, in a nearby vacant cheese factory. They may have been selling the parcels on the black market, consuming the contents themselves, or turning some of the loot over to the German High Command. Gene would never learn the truth. However, it was "plain as day" to him none of his jailers appeared to be skipping any meals.

Designated the group leader of his 20-man parcel-sharing platoon, Gene faced the unenviable prospect of dividing each parcel into 20 equal shares. The procedure was the same each time. He would set the package on a wood-slatted table and begin the division process. It was easy to split up the cigarettes, as there were 20 in a pack. The chocolate was more problematic. The chocolate bar was about an inch thick and segmented into bite-sized pieces—except there weren't 20 segments, resulting in 20, roughly equal, broken bits if they chose to divide it rather than use it for bartering.

Toilet tissue distribution was easy, as it consisted of 20 sheets packed in neat rows of five sheets deep and four across. Crackers and other items had to be physically split up, for which Gene would borrow a small knife one of the men kept hidden in his bunk. The group decided not to break up the bar of soap, for it was more valuable as trade material with the München housewives who were always eager to trade bread for soap. Throughout the entire time Gene would be divvying up the parcel there were 19 hungry sets of eyes watching his every motion, anxious for him to finish. Gene did feel some pressure but was patient and took his time to carefully cut up the chocolate, crackers, and other not-so-easy-to-divide as neatly as he could.

There was a can of spam or bacon which the Germans would cut open in advance. The resulting problem was the meat needed to be quickly consumed and after dividing it into 20 pieces they would, in fact, immediately eat it. Gene assumed his captors feared the prisoners would stash unopened cans into a stockpile to use in potential escape attempts.

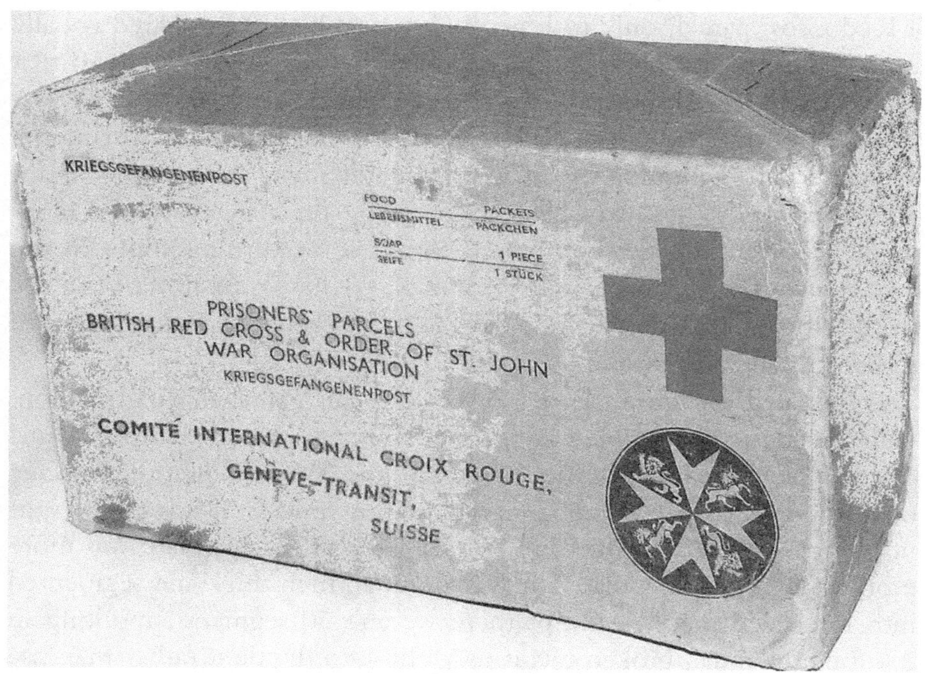

A World War II Red Cross parcel.

There was also a small Red Cross ration of sugar, prunes, and powdered milk. They decided to accumulate those items until they had enough to make "ice cream" by combining them with snow. The resulting concoction was so rich they would all get upset stomachs from it. Despite the stomach aches they would repeat the process again and again as the taste delight was worth the pain and the subsequent affliction Gene referred to as "the squirts."

One day after distributing the Red Cross parcel Gene noticed an enterprising prisoner picking out little bits of tobacco from between the slats in the table top. He worked at it all morning until he had just enough tobacco to roll it into a sliver of newspaper which he intended to serve as cigarette paper. Once finished, he put the miniature cigarette between his lips, lit it and squealed in pain; for when he inhaled, the lighted cigarette was sucked into his mouth, giving him a good burn. Everyone witnessing the episode got a solid laugh at his expense.

While Gene thought the American prisoners had it bad, he soon discovered the Russian prisoners of war were far worse off. One morning Gene was milling around the grounds with a few of his fellow POWs when they noticed a column of about a thousand recently captured Russian prisoners being marched into the Russian compound. Earlier in the morning the Germans had locked the existing Russian prisoners into their barracks and Gene was about to learn why they had done so.

The newly arriving Russians were directed into a series of about 10 single-file lines, each line leading to a table where they were given cursory physical examinations. After each prisoner completed his exam he was directed to join one of two groups being congregated in opposite corners of the compound. The process consumed most of the day and provided the American POWs with something to do. It was mid-afternoon when the Germans completed the examinations. They escorted a group of prisoners who had been segregated in one corner of the compound into various barracks until only the second group remained.

Gene had been watching the progress all day when one of the veteran American prisoners poked him in the ribs and said: "Watch what happens next."

Gene looked at him quizzically and continued to observe the events unfolding in the Russian compound.

About half an hour later a large number of black uniformed "SS" soldiers, each armed with a machine gun, entered the compound in a hurry and quickly formed a picket line opposite the remaining group of about 500 Russians. They proceeded to organize them into a marching column, four across, and escorted them out of the camp and in the direction of a meadow located not more than a couple hundred yards away, near where a few transport trucks were parked. To the Russians it probably appeared as if they were about to be moved elsewhere. The tree line partially obscured the meadow from full view of the American compound but was not dense enough to prevent some stray bullets from reaching the camp during the ensuing slaughter.

Gene began to feel sick when he noticed the prisoners standing around him were hitting the ground. Out of instinct he did the same as the Germans proceeded to open fire on the defenseless Russians. What began as a chorus of screams from the helpless Russians slowly whittled down to that of a soloist; then it went eerily silent.

Within moments the silence was interrupted by the distinctive metal-on-metal clanking of soldiers reloading their weapons and the odd moan or two. Single rifle or pistol shots would ring out for another couple of minutes until a calm, not unlike a calm following a storm, settled in.

With the last of them dispatched, the Germans unlocked the barracks and forced a number of Russians into a makeshift burial detail. Gene and his fellow prisoners slowly began to wander away from the side of their compound facing the Russians. The same prisoner who had been standing next to him earlier struck up a one-sided conversation as they walked back toward their barracks. "Ya gotta understand the Kraut way of thinking. It's a matter they consider the Russkies to be subhuman. It's almost like they believe they're doing the poor bastards a favor by killing 'em. Ya know, Russia didn't sign no Geneva Convention so the Krauts think they can do anything they want to 'em. If you ask me, the guys they just shot are better off."

"What do you mean?" Gene asked.

"Listen Mack, compared to what they feed those Russkies, it's like we're stayin' at the Ritz!"

Gene couldn't think of anything to say as he slowly walked over to the far side of the American compound, as if putting distance between himself and the slaughter might ease the emotional trauma he was experiencing.

It wasn't long before Gene learned the Germans considered the Stalag to be a "work camp" where able-bodied men were forced into slave-labor pools. There was an almost negligible increase in rations when assigned to a work pool and certainly not enough to offset the increase in physical and psychological stresses which accompanied the chores. Nobody was offered a choice: it was either work or punishment. In their physical condition, punishment was almost tantamount to a death sentence.

He soon found himself in a near-daily routine of marching 1 mile to a railroad siding which ran alongside the town of Moosburg, immediately adjacent the camp. The march never began until after dark, when they were safe from marauding fighter planes. Once at the railway siding he and his fellow prisoners would climb aboard boxcars for the 37-mile train ride to München.

Most of the guards accompanying them on the trip were older or suffering from war injuries. Consequently, it was necessary for Gene and his fellow prisoners to give them a boost up into the railcar. The guard would first pass his rifle to one of the prisoners standing in the railcar doorway; a couple of men would then grab hold of his waist and boost him up into the car. He'd take back his rifle and make himself comfortable sitting on the wood floor opposite the open door.

For the most part the guards were reasonably friendly. If not for the German manpower shortage, most of them probably would have been home as a result of their wartime injuries. Gene concluded the injuries kept them out of the fighting and may have saved their lives.

The Germans timed the train ride so they would arrive at first light, before Allied air power might intervene. He never knew what manner of assignment awaited him and it largely depended upon whether München had been targeted by Allied bombers the day, or night, prior. On more than one occasion he found himself in a mad dash to seek out whatever manner of cover he could find when the Americans targeted München for a daylight raid.

He often worked clearing damage in the railway yards as the railroad was a priority of the German High Command. Sometimes the routine would change and he would be sent into München proper. It was on one such assignment he faced the grisly sight of a British airman who had apparently been blown from the wreckage of his bomber. Only the lower half of the man remained and it was mashed against a brick wall, maybe three stories high, as if glued there by his own blood. A section of landing gear lay upside down in the center of the boulevard. Upon Gene's return from the day's work the body was still plastered against the wall. However, the landing gear had been removed from the street. There was no pity from the populace for any Allied airmen or soldiers.

Members of the work details in München, unlike the men left behind at the Stalag, were fed lunch. When it was time for a lunch break the guards would take the prisoners behind a nearby restaurant where a number of crudely constructed picnic-style wooden tables awaited them.

Lunch was always served to Gene and his fellow slave-laborers outdoors, without regard to weather conditions. The guards, on the other hand, would walk to the front of the restaurant, sit at tables inside, and order their meals from the limited menu offered on any particular day. Though they could certainly smell what was cooking in the kitchen, the prisoners were not privy to the menu. The aroma of food cooking only a few feet away dramatically amplified the gnawing feeling in their stomachs.

The kitchen crew would bring Gene and his companions a bowl of soup, usually something they referred to as "barley soup," and a slice of black bread which was barely more than colored sawdust held together by glue. One day, out of curiosity, Gene put a match to a small piece of bread. It burned blueish-green! The combination of the soup and combustible bread often resulted in the men suffering from severe cases of flatulence. Later in the evening the resulting digestive disorder, according to Gene, "would further enhance" the stench in the barracks.

Clearing bomb damage was grueling work and involved a great deal of heavy lifting. Gene was fortunate: on his first excursion into München he was able to trade five cigarettes for a pair of work gloves or his hands would have soon been covered with bleeding sores. The crudely crafted mittens he and most of his fellow prisoners wore would have quickly disintegrated from the rugged use. One of the more veteran prisoners had tipped him off in advance to the fact he'd want to bring five cigarettes so he could trade for what would quickly prove to be badly needed work gloves. Gene didn't smoke, which made the accumulation of cigarettes an easier task.

There were also "political" prisoners working in München. Clothed in vertically striped uniforms constructed from paper-thin material, they were not allowed to possess gloves. Gene noticed their hands were discolored and swollen. Interacting with them was strictly prohibited, and they were carefully segregated from the prisoners of war. Gene concluded the political prisoners were apparently considered expendable and, as time wore on, their numbers steadily declined. He considered the political prisoners to be worse off than the Russians.

It was not uncommon during the course of a 12-hour work day in München for one of the Russian or political prisoners to crumple in a heap. It was all the excuse the guards required to shoot them on the spot. However, each time it happened to one of the Western Allies the collapsed man would be immediately brought to his feet and propped up by his fellow prisoners until he could regain his footing. The reality was not all of the guards were old and friendly. A handful of the guards required very little reason to shoot a prisoner and a few of them appeared to enjoy it.

One morning they had crossed the Isar River and were walking past the Faber factory. Bottles of ink and fountain pens had poured out of a bombed-out supply truck, drawing Gene's attention. He filled his pockets with as many bottles of ink as he could manage and a handful of fountain pens, knowing he could use them for his sketches as well as for bartering material. When he returned to the Stalag the same night he proceeded to paint an ink drawing on the back of his battle jacket of a familiar roadside sign from his days in DeKalb—the DeKalb "flying ear of corn."

It wasn't long before his "flying ear of corn" caught the attention of another prisoner, who also happened to be from the DeKalb area. Although they didn't know each other, simply being able to share some memories of places they both had visited brought them a little psychological relief. Gene thought to himself the world truly was growing smaller.

On one of his numerous forced excursions into München, Gene was part of a prison crew working to repair a bomb-damaged road critical to serving the beleaguered city. The bombed-out section was more than a mile outside of München proper and took them some time to reach. Upon his arrival he discovered the inbound side of the road was interrupted by a series of bomb craters. He knew it was going to be a

The "Winged Ear" was a common sight up and down the highways around DeKalb, Illinois, where most farmers purchased their seed from DeKalb Seed Company.

long, strenuous day for it required a tremendous effort to fill and compact the craters without the benefit of heavy equipment.

While working on the road a covered troop transport bounded past them, and as it did so, five or six bodies were pitched out the back of the truck. Gene watched in horror as the bodies, clad in vertical-striped uniforms, rolled along the highway. When he realized some of victims weren't dead he and another prisoner started to move toward them. One of the nearby guards immediately fired his rifle into the air, bringing the two men to an abrupt halt.

Gene motioned to the injured people who were pitifully moaning as they struggled to crawl to the side of the road, away from potential traffic.

"*Nein! Nein! Sie Juden!*" the guard shouted, stopping him in his tracks.

Gene watched in horror as the guard proceeded to execute the injured persons with his rifle. Gene was so enraged he wanted to kill him. As he considered taking action he quickly glanced around, only to realize the rifle shots had attracted the attention of additional nearby guards, several of whom, rifles at the ready, were running in his direction. His survival instincts dictated he put his head down and return to work.

About an hour later when, in Gene's words, "things had calmed down a bit," one of the guards explained to him the unfortunate souls who were tossed from the truck were slave-laborers. They "were no longer productive." The word "productive" stuck in his head. For him it was a key to understanding the Germans and how to survive captivity at their hands. Over the course of his "employment" in München he would witness the above scene again, including one time when he was in a railcar coming to a stop prior to unloading. It proved to be a stomach-wrenching start to the day and a further reminder as to why he was in the war in the first place.

If he wasn't assigned to clearing roads or the railway station, then he might be digging dead bodies from the rubble of bombed-out buildings. When he was searching for dead bodies he quickly learned to keep an eye out for grieving civilians, as they were prone to throw bricks at him and his fellow prisoners.

The majority of the dead were women and children and the occasional older man. Excavating their remains and gently placing them into carts, pulled by fellow prisoners, for transport to the cemetery, was mentally tough to withstand and the assignment he despised the most. He saw more dead children than living ones in München. He assumed the children were either in school, had been shipped to safe locations in the countryside, or killed while huddling with their families during bombing raids.

While the work itself varied from back-breaking to heart-wrenching, there were occasional moments of humor, as when Gene discovered aerial bombs could leave strange results. A building could be completely leveled by a bomb strike, but just as often only the outside wall would be peeled off, leaving a doll-house effect revealing intact and inhabited "doll-house" apartments. While marching to or from his work assignment he'd glance up and notice doll-house residents looking down at him, seldom acknowledging his passing, but always staring as if they'd never seen the prisoner procession before. They appeared to him as if they lacked all semblance of emotion.

Unexploded bombs were a problem, as they were often buried underneath the rubble of damaged structures and not easily discovered. It was not unusual for a prisoner to inadvertently detonate a bomb, killing him and anyone within range. The additional element of danger added to the stress, not to mention the U.S. Army Air Corps practice of daylight-bombing München while Gene was laboring there. POWs were not allowed into the bomb shelters so they sheltered as best they could and prayed. He was keenly aware he could be killed at just about any time with little or no notice. Consequently, the stress never eased up, nor did the gnawing feeling in his stomach.

On one occasion Gene was working on the seventh floor of a doll-house building, clearing apartments of rubble and any furnishings damaged beyond repair. The procedure was to throw the rubble and damaged furniture down to the street where other prisoners loaded the debris onto carts. There were no horses to pull the carts, leaving the job to the prisoners.

Gene entered a seventh-floor apartment and discovered an intact Steinway grand piano. He sat down and played a few songs to the delight of his fellow prisoners and, to a lesser extent, the German guards. He had been playing for about 10 minutes when an idea struck him. He glanced down at the street and noticed the guard was no longer paying any attention to him. Thinking to himself he'd never have this opportunity again, he decided to push the Steinway over the edge and send it crashing into the rubble and pavement below. Not only did it cause a deafening semi-musical racket when it smashed into the ground; it also produced a suffocating cloud of dust, totally immersing the guard from head to toe.

The guard began shrieking obscenities, as everyone who witnessed the event, including other nearby guards, laughed. Gene was long gone by the time the dusty guard reached the seventh floor in search of the piano-dumping culprit.

For reasons Gene still cannot explain, shortly after the piano incident he worked his way back to street level and decided, in his words, "to take a walk right up the center of the boulevard." He found himself fascinated by what remained of the "beautiful München architecture" and "stately Victorian houses" while slowly walking away from his work detail. He was inexplicably oblivious to his situation and was basically sightseeing. He walked for about four blocks and had just turned around to return when he heard a familiar German-accented word:

"Halt!"

Gene snapped back to reality; a number of civilians had apparently noticed his sightseeing excursion and sought the attention of one of the guards, who was quickly running toward him. When the guard caught up with him he slapped Gene across the right cheek several times with his gloved hand while yelling a stream of obscenities. Gene meekly accepted the punishment, lest he risk the guard losing his self-control. The aggravated German escorted him back to his station and remained near his side the balance of the day. Gene concluded the guard would have had a difficult time explaining the escape of a prisoner and was taking no chances.

Even now, many decades later, Gene cannot explain what he was thinking when he wandered off and wonders why the guard didn't simply shoot him—he would have been justified in assuming Gene was attempting an escape. Not only did the guard stay by his side the remainder of the day, but he also accompanied him on the return train ride to VII-A. Gene prefers to believe the guard remained with him more for his own protection than for the reason he might try to wander off again or otherwise cause him grief.

One morning, following a Royal Air Force overnight incendiary bomb attack, Gene was walking past the München zoo. Unfortunately the zoo had also been a victim of the incendiary attack and numerous fires burned throughout it. A distressed elephant was slowly rocking back and forth, smoke pouring from his hide in five or six locations as phosphorous from the bombing raid slowly burned deeper into his massive body. Gene felt sorry for the elephant and didn't understand why the zoo had not been evacuated. It also appeared to him there were no zookeepers to relieve the poor animal either. He concluded the zoo animals were even lower on the transportation and care totem pole than were Gene and his fellow prisoners or they'd have been vacated long ago.

On another morning, as he was being marched to the day's workplace, he noticed eight young women, each holding a baby in their arms. They were standing side by side and a number of onlookers were present. A small group of local officials wearing Nazi armbands was presenting each of the young mothers with a medal. In a subdued voice one of the guards explained to him what was transpiring.

"Those are Hitler's Brides. The babies are pure Aryan. With so many of the men gone it falls to the 'SS' to keep the population from disappearing. That party official is presenting them with a medal for their efforts."

"What?" Gene asked, not certain he understood.

"Ja, it is a tradition going back to the old days of the big Nazi Party celebrations in Nuremberg. The brides must prove they are 100 percent Aryan and are encouraged to have babies with 'SS' officers to assure purity." The guard paused and shrugged his shoulders. "It is the Nazi way."

Gene thought for a moment and asked: "Are you a Nazi?"

"*Nein! Nein!*" Replied the guard, his voice barely above a whisper. He proceeded to urge the work-gang to move along in response to the sudden appearance of a pair of Gestapo agents.

For the most part the guards on the work details and at the camp were older and somewhat friendly, or at least as friendly as they dared be. Regardless of whether they were "SS" or Wehrmacht, all of them were confounded as to the reason why the Americans were fighting the

A "Lebensborn" medal. Translated: "Brightness shall be us. Every mother good blood."

Germans instead of the Russians, which always provoked some lively discussions. Some guards kept to themselves and didn't engage in casual conversation or barter with the prisoners. To Gene most of the guards appeared to be biding their time while awaiting an end to the war so they could return home. It was unusual for any guard to exhibit unwarranted violence, except when it came to the Russians.

Many of the sentries would engage in some limited bartering with the prisoners, usually for American cigarettes. Early in his stay at VII-A, Gene swapped the cigarettes he managed to accumulate for drawing materials and began compiling a collection of sketches and cartoons he'd create to help him make it through the weeks and months. Most of the sketches were reflections on the events he was witnessing, though he still managed a few of his always-in-demand cartoons. He possessed a keen eye and an even keener sense of humor. By the time liberation was drawing near, his pencil drawings completely filled two sketchbooks.

Work details consumed most of the daylight hours of each work day. There was no early return to camp; trains would only travel after sunset in deference to Allied air power. Simply making it through each day alive was all Gene and his fellow prisoners could hope to achieve.

Following the return train ride to Moosburg, where it might be as late as 2300 hours, it was necessary for the prisoners, accompanied by their

A bombed-out German railway yard.

guards, to make the 1-mile walk back to the camp. The guards would intentionally skirt the center of town, even though it would have been the most direct route. Their intention was to prevent any interaction, such as bartering, between the prisoners and the local populace.

The work detail marches through München, unlike those through Moosburg, presented an opportunity to trade with the local München women. A bar of soap could fetch four loaves of bread to share among Gene's Red Cross ration group of 20 men. The extra bread wasn't enough to make a meaningful difference but it helped keep them alive another day, for staying alive one more day was a shared goal. Gene quickly learned the phrase: "*Seife für Brot,*" "Soap for bread." Of course the bread was only marginally better than what they experienced at the Stalag; the civilians were desperately short of flour and would extend their flour supplies with sawdust. The sawdust supplement had the practical effect of filling their stomachs and thereby easing the hunger pains.

One night, as they trekked toward their Stalag after a long day of forced labor, word spread through the line the Germans were body-searching all of the prisoners as they reached the front gate. Everything they might have picked up in München during the course of the workday, mostly loaves of bread from bartering along with radio parts and assorted odds and ends, was being confiscated. Gene had traded soap for bread earlier in the day and quickly dispersed the loaves to the men around him. They all ate as much as they could stomach rather than allow the Germans to steal it for themselves.

Just in time for Christmas 1944 morale began to sink to new lows as hundreds of recently captured Americans began entering the camp several times a day. They brought with them stories of a massive German offensive in the Ardennes with "hundreds of Tiger tanks." They told stories about how the Germans were splitting the Allied armies in two halves. More alarming still was the nature of the prisoners themselves as their ranks included the regular army, tank crews, cooks, doctors, and even an entire marching band. Several engineer-linemen marched in while still wearing their tool belts complete with, of all things, wire cutters.

All of them had only recently been taken prisoner and recited the same story of having found themselves helpless in the face of overwhelming odds. Many were in awe of the latest type of German tank, one even larger than the dreaded Tiger. They commiserated over the fact their anti-tank shells had harmlessly bounced off the new "King Tiger" tanks. Gene, having witnessed the death and misery in München, couldn't understand how the Germans could suddenly be winning the war.

Up until then newly arriving prisoners brought with them news of continuous victories in the field, instilling hope in Gene and his fellow prisoners the war would soon end. When, in Gene's words, "an entire marching band" filed into camp, all hope for a quick Allied victory disappeared. After all, marching bands were in the rear, safely away from the front lines. Yet there they were, walking straight into Stalag VII-A. Gene would never forget the despair he felt when he witnessed their arrival.

With the war having taken an unexpected turn for the worse, entirely dampening Christmas-week spirits, the British prisoners announced they were putting on a stage production and the Americans were being invited to attend their premier performance. The Brits titled their production *The*

Germans advancing in the early stages of the Battle of the Bulge. The winter of 1944–45 was one of the most severe on record at the time.

Barretts of Wimple Street, a play about a woman trying to find husbands for her three daughters. Gene and his fellow POWs were dubious and a number of them chose not to partake. Gene determined the pending performance could present an opportunity to break up the drudgery of his daily routine and decided he'd attend.

When the time arrived to walk over to the British compound a couple dozen German guards appeared and escorted the Americans into one of the British barracks. The barracks had been cleared of all furnishings except for numerous rows of benches to seat the audience. There was a surprisingly well-constructed, elevated stage platform situated at the front of the room.

Gene considered the Brits had done a remarkable job stitching together a curtain and improvising some pretty respectable stage lighting. In his opinion the room did bear a reasonably good resemblance to a British playhouse and he anticipated a fun performance. Guards were stationed approximately every 10 feet along the walls and appeared to be genuinely curious about what the Brits were up to, paying little attention to the American audience.

Gene was sitting in the front row when the curtain rose. A British soldier, dressed as a middle-aged female, daintily strolled into the middle of the stage and explained her name was "Mother." Mother was wearing heavily applied make-up and wore a stylishly long dress, down to her ankles, with highly polished, black high-heeled shoes. She was immediately greeted by a cascade of whistles and cat-calls.

Mother displayed remarkable patience as she waited for the audience to quiet down. Once satisfied she had the proper atmosphere established, she proceeded with the script and explained the play would relate her efforts in obtaining suitable husbands for her three daughters. First, however, she was going to introduce her daughters to the audience one at a time.

Gene looked around the room and noticed all of the guards were staring at Mother. He wasn't sure if they were engaged in the performance or stunned at the Brit's proficiency with make-up. Mother made herself comfortable in an armchair placed centerstage as she prepared to introduce her daughters.

In a few moments the first daughter strode onto the stage dressed in a sexy dress and red high heels, wearing a remarkable quantity of make-up and topped by a bright blonde wig. Her hair cascaded down onto her shoulders. As she gracefully walked up to Mother, she drew a renewed round of whistles and cat-calls. Some of the men were calling her "cutie pie" and urging her to join the audience. A few of the men hollered rather unsavory descriptions of her which were less than flattering.

Mother expended a gallant effort as she struggled to return the audience to a state of relative quiet. She found it necessary to soundly berate them and threatened to stop the performance right then and there. The crowd immediately went nearly dead-silent.

Satisfied, Mother proceeded to introduce daughter number two. Daughter number two, a red-head with hair draped across her shoulders and half-way down her chest, received an even louder and more rudely laced reception than did the first. Some of the men shouted out how "darn good looking" the girls were, though not always in such gentile terms.

Gene commented to the man sitting beside him: "The Brits certainly have a hell of a knack for costumes and make-up." Smiling, the fellow prisoner replied with a simple, "Yep!"

Again, Mother waited for silence and proceeded to introduce daughter number three, a soldier who appeared to be not more than 18 years of age and equally made-up. His dress was a bit shorter than the others and his blonde wig sported tightly curled, long hair. He was, in Gene's opinion, the "cutest one" and received a relentless stream of whistles and propositions. No matter the efforts of Mother to regain control of the crowd; the heckling and sexually evocative ideas being offered from the audience did not cease. Eventually Mother gave up and dropped the curtain which came down with a notable thud.

She appeared from behind the curtain and raised her voice as loud as she could while remaining in her role:

"Alright you Yanks! Go on home now, the show's over for you."

The guards, caught unaware, had no idea what was transpiring and grew nervous at the sight of all the men suddenly moving toward the door at the same time. It took them a few moments to comprehend the performance was over. While the show for the "Yanks" did not go on, Gene and his companions had been placed into a relatively good mood at the expense of the Brits. To this day he regrets not being able to watch the entire play as he knew his British companions had put a tremendous effort into it and the show had meaning for them. He can still visualize the pissed-off Brits standing on the stage, staring at the "damned Yanks" as he left the room.

The following day, December 24, 1944, Gene returned to the München rail yards to clear bomb damage. It was an overcast, cold, miserable day. Shortly before the lunchtime work-break a German staff car carrying a Wehrmacht colonel came bounding up the roadway alongside the railroad tracks, causing him to stop working and check it out. Staff cars were few and far between in Gene's München experiences and the fact the colonel had the clout to warrant a staff car meant he was likely well connected, raising Gene's curiosity level all the more.

The staff car skidded to an abrupt halt about 20 feet from Gene and his workmate, coming to a rest directly alongside a pair of black GIs who were diligently working on the rails. The colonel literally leapt from the staff car and swiftly walked over to one of the two men, both of whom were privates. The two African-American soldiers had ceased working and were leaning on their shovels, casually watching as the colonel approached.

The colonel and one of the privates, a particularly tall man, proceeded to engage in an animated conversation. The colonel's English was limited, requiring both men to make extensive use of sign language. Gene quickly deciphered what they were talking about and learned the prisoner was in possession of something the men commonly referred to as a "D" bar, or chocolate bar. The colonel had somehow learned of it and was offering him what, to Gene, was the unheard-of swap of 10 loaves of bread in exchange for the "D" bar. The colonel was appealing to the man's sense of family as he pointed out the next day was Christmas and he had no present for his little girl. He desired to make the "D" bar a Christmas gift for his daughter.

Gene was growing concerned for the private's life as he was absolutely refusing the trade. The reality was the colonel could have simply confiscated the "D" bar and nobody would have been able to stop him. To his credit he made no such attempt. After additional negotiating the colonel shook his head up and down a few times, apparently agreeing to a counter-proposal. He returned to the staff car and disappeared.

About 30 minutes later the colonel returned; however, instead of being in the company of only a driver, he was accompanied by three armed soldiers sitting in the rear seat, rifles at their sides. As the colonel and his men exited the car it was apparent to Gene the soldiers were carrying loaves of bread, having left their rifles behind them. A smiling colonel accepted the chocolate bar and the private and his pal began stuffing what looked like at least 12 loaves into their pockets. In fact, there were so many loaves they had to fashion a makeshift bag out of one of their jackets to hold the balance of their Christmas loot.

The two lucky soldiers waved goodbye as the colonel sped off, his mission accomplished. Gene formed an image of a little blonde German girl wearing a huge smile as she unwrapped her chocolate bar Christmas present the following morning.

The next day was Christmas and the Germans presented Gene's barracks with a present—a "huge wheel of cheese." The prisoners appointed a couple of men to divvy up the cheese, which was labeled as having originated in Argentina. Once they finished carefully cutting out the portion of the wheel infested with maggots, each of the men received a small block of cheese as an unexpected Christmas treat.

January 1, 1945, ushered in a seemingly endless procession of Russian prisoners, further overfilling the Russian compound and magnifying the food shortage for the Russians. By comparison, Gene and his fellow prisoners were living the life fantastic.

Gene was milling around one morning and noticed the Germans were rounding up approximately 500 Russian prisoners and marching them out of the compound. The procession drew an audience from the British, French, and American compounds as they watched the Germans march the Russians into a meadow perhaps 200 yards away and just out of direct sight of the Stalag. The day prior the Germans had forced the Russians to construct a barbed-wire enclosure surrounding the same meadow and it soon became alarmingly obvious what manner of evil they had been planning.

Once all of the Russians were in the meadow the Germans brought out massive rolls of barbed wire and closed off the entrance. The Russians were not wearing coats as the Germans routinely confiscated all winter garments from them. Many of them didn't even possess boots or shoes. The Germans left a few guards behind and returned to their warm barracks, leaving the Russians to freeze to death. The same meadow which had been the site of mass murder by machine-gun fire had been transformed into an open-air death sentence.

The following morning Gene joined a group of fellow POWs gathered near the edge of the compound, closest to the meadow. It was obvious many of the Russians were still alive, despite the bitter cold, as the sounds of moans and crying could be heard. A few of the German guards were joking and laughing within easy earshot of the dying Russians. Gene wished he had been given a work assignment in München that day, taking him away from the grisly scene. It was a scene his German captors would repeat over and over again.

Gene and one of his friends engaged in a conversation with a German guard about the Russian prisoner situation. He was a decorated veteran and wore, among other medals and a ribbon, an award indicating he was a participant in the devastating "Winter War" of 1941–42. The guard explained what the Germans were doing in a tone of voice completely absent of compassion.

"We put the most troublesome of the Russians into the gulag until they die. Once they are all kaput we force more of them into the gulag to bury their dead comrades as best as they can. Naturally it takes them all day to dig the graves because the ground is basically frozen and so much labor leaves them in a weakened condition. We will, of course, leave the burial detail locked in the gulag until they also die. We continue to repeat the process until the Russians have learned their lesson." The guard did not expand on what he meant by "learned their lesson," nor did Gene feel there was any point in pursuing it.

No sooner had the German guard finished his account than the sound of an airplane's engine redirected everyone's attention. Flying overhead in a lazy circle around the sprawling camp was an American P-51 Mustang fighter plane. The pilot proceeded to make several passes over the camp, rocking his wings each time. A spontaneous cheer erupted from everyone, for then, with certainty, they knew the Allies were aware of their location.

CHAPTER SEVENTEEN

Hans Schwaniger

Gene suspected the Germans had planted spies among the prisoners for the specific purpose of uncovering Jewish soldiers. From time to time a guard would enter the barracks calling out the name of a prisoner. Once identified the guard would request the prisoner go with him, but he was to leave his belongings behind, as the guard would advise him, in a nonchalant manner, he would "return soon." Those prisoners never returned and they were almost always Jewish.

Gene figured the Germans had somehow decided the Geneva Convention didn't apply to Jewish/American prisoners of war. After thinking about it a little more he realized some of the questions he'd been asked back at Stalag XII-A were "loaded" and were probably intended to reveal as much about each prisoner's ethnic background as possible. He would soon discover some of the questions posed to him regarding his prewar job history could impact where a prisoner might eventually be dispatched.

One morning Gene had been shooting the breeze with a friend when a German corporal, with whom Gene had done some bartering, entered the barracks and loudly announced: "Metcalfe! Eugene Metcalfe! Stand up!"

When they heard Gene's name called his friend tapped him on the leg and shook his head back and forth, meaning Gene shouldn't answer. Gene turned to face the opposite direction and pretended not to have heard anything. Gene assumed the Germans had decided he was Jewish and was destined to join the legion of the "never-to-return." Chills ran up and down his spine as the corporal continued to announce his name while making his way through the barracks and displaying a photo of Gene taken at Stalag XII-A. Gene didn't answer; however, the corporal knew Gene and upon finding him he firmly kicked Gene's boot and asked: "Herr Metcalfe, why didn't you answer me? I've called your name at least six times!" There was no animosity in his voice; in fact, he sounded a bit as if his feelings had been hurt.

Gene pointed to his right ear and said, "Sorry corporal, I'm deaf in this ear and didn't hear you."

"*Ja, ja,* I remember." The corporal motioned with his arms as he ordered: "Assemble your belongings and come with me."

As Gene stuffed his duffle bag he realized this was different. If they were going to kill him, he reasoned, they'd have told him to leave his gear behind as was their custom when a prisoner was on, what the POWs called, "a one-way ticket" out. He and the corporal walked to the main gate where the corporal produced a Red Cross parcel, held it out to Gene and said: "This is yours."

Gene had just been presented with an entire Red Cross parcel for himself. It was a strict rule Red Cross parcels be shared among 20 men so it was more than just an unexpected treat; it was without precedent. To put it mildly, he was shocked.

Once they were outside the Stalag the corporal handed him a cigarette and actually lit it for him. He proceeded to explain the day's itinerary by telling him they were going to board a civilian train because he had been ordered to take Gene to a farm outside of Landshut where he would stay and work.

"I'm going to work on a farm? Are you kidding me?" Gene's question caused the corporal to stop in his tracks.

"You're a *Bauer, ja?*" the corporal asked.

"What's a *Bauer?*" Gene replied.

The corporal smiled and motioned for Gene to resume walking. As they continued toward the railway station in Moosburg, the corporal explained the situation.

"*Bauer* ... a farm worker, understand?"

At first Gene didn't know how to respond. Then he remembered he had told the interrogator at Stalag XII-A he had been a farmer in civilian life. He nodded his head in the affirmative and replied: "*Ja,* I'm a *Bauer,* for sure.*"* He breathed a sigh of relief, knowing he was not embarking on a one-way trip from which there was no return.

"*Gut!*" the guard replied.

His guard explained they would be traveling to a "Bauernhof" outside of Landshut where Gene would be living with a farmer and his family and help them with the farming. He told Gene he would be leaving him with the farmer. The corporal was friendly in his demeanor and perhaps looking forward to a little time away from the camp. They had frequently bartered with one another and Gene knew the man to be married with young children. He was also a veteran of the "Winter War" and somewhat hobbled by his war wounds.

The little lie Gene told the interrogator at Stalag XII-A about being a farmer was getting Gene out of a hell-hole and onto a small farm situated somewhere in the general vicinity of Landshut, Germany. The lie may well have saved him from death by starvation or bombing.

Upon reaching the railway depot the two men discovered it would be several hours before the train would arrive so they decided to wait inside. Eventually a train pulled up and proved to be fairly overcrowded with an assortment of civilians and soldiers returning home on leave. There were no antiaircraft guns protecting the train and Gene hoped the reason for the lack of guns was because Allied planes were not likely to attack trainloads of civilians.

They had been traveling for less than two hours when Gene noticed a P-47 Thunderbolt fighter plane flying low and parallel to the train. Gene's eyes opened wide at the sight of the fighter and he shoved the corporal's shoulder, hard, several times. When the corporal turned around Gene pointed out the window. Realizing they were about to be attacked the corporal shouted out what sounded like "*Flieger, oh Scheisse!*" He immediately leapt from his seat and yanked hard and long on the emergency cord, forcing the train to come to a very abrupt stop.

Even before the train came to a complete halt, all of the passengers began jumping out and running for whatever cover they could find. Unfortunately, the fleeing passengers were caught in the middle of an expansive, open meadow where there was little protective cover. The corporal ordered Gene to remain in his seat and stay next to the window while he ran for it. The corporal found a little cover in a small depression where he proceeded to aim his rifle at Gene, who was still clinging to his Red Cross parcel.

Gene looked out the window, desperately searching the sky for signs of the P-47. For a moment he thought the plane had moved on until he spotted it maneuvering into position to strafe the train with its machine guns. Fortunately for Gene there were no rockets or bombs strapped to the plane's wings. The passenger car provided absolutely no protection and, no matter what angle the pilot chose for his attack, he could easily be killed. He glanced over at the guard who was lying prone on the ground with his rifle aimed directly at Gene.

Gene decided this was probably the end of the line; there was no way he could survive the pending attack. He began to shovel the contents of the Red Cross parcel into his mouth as if there would be no tomorrow, which in fact, he justly believed to be the event.

As the sound of the P-47 grew louder Gene buried his head into the seat facing him while he continued to vigorously consume the foodstuffs. He heard a short burst of machine-gun fire but at the last moment the pilot apparently realized it was a civilian train and therefore didn't offer much in terms of military value. He ceased firing then swung his plane around and targeted the engine with devastating results. Hundreds of holes appeared in the engine housing, gushing fierce eruptions of steam. Gene peeked out the window and realized the engine had been completely destroyed. He watched as the plane made a final fly-over then disappeared into the horizon. Though the attack was over, many of the women and children were still screaming hysterically.

Relieved he wasn't going to die after all, Gene was ticked off at himself for stuffing most of the contents of the Red Cross parcel into his shrunken stomach. His "feeding frenzy" left him with a very angry and upset belly and no goodies for later. With the engine destroyed, they found it necessary to walk the remainder of the way to the farm. The corporal explained he had lived near there before the war and it would not be a hard walk once they reached the road, which was not far from them.

The road he referred to was barely more than a dirt cart path as they trudged onwards into the early evening. When they finally arrived at

Hans Schwaniger's Tyrolean cap was the worse for wear.

the farm, the corporal spoke a few words to the farmer and his wife. Apparently satisfied with the arrangement, the farmer bid the corporal, "*Gute Nacht*," to which he responded with, "*Auf Wiedersehen*." The corporal turned to Gene and said: "I leave you now and will return for you come summertime." He turned back up the road and slowly disappeared into the rapidly approaching darkness.

Hans Schwaniger, the farmer, was a short, skinny man with a large, bright white, handle-bar moustache accentuating his narrow, drawn face. He had light brown hair, streaked with white, and wore a gray Tyrolean cap. His wife was more than two times his size and commanded about a 3-inch height advantage over him. Her long, blonde, fading-into-gray hair was pulled back into a tight bun. Her pudgy cheeks were bright red and her lips were pursed into a frown as she stared at the new arrival.

Gene's new hosts occupied one of about 14 or 15 small farm houses situated just beyond the walls of an ancient castle, once the domain of a local baron and currently owned by his heirs. It was described to Gene as "Baron Rickenhaslaw's castle," while the locals referred to it simply as "Rickenhaslaw Castle." Situated on a hill above the Inn River, within its walls were a gazebo, which served as the center of social activity on Sundays, and a small Catholic chapel. Just beyond an expansive courtyard was the cemetery, cordoned off into its own section. It appeared to have been there for centuries and sat alongside a stone cliff.

There was a manmade cave carved into the rock and protected by huge, carved wooden doors. Within the cave a series of roughly demarked storage areas had been created by painting lines on the stone floor, marking off storage space reserved for each farmer. The farmers would stockpile potatoes, carrots, beets, cabbages, canned goods, and similar foodstuffs in the cool, dark confines of the cave where they were safe from the elements.

It was an honor system created over many generations and strictly respected. Hans knew if he had 90 potatoes in his storage area he could return in a month, for example, and his 90 potatoes would still be there. Nobody had refrigeration or much storage space within their small homes, so the cave fulfilled many of the farmers' long- and short-term storage needs. Gene was amazed the honor system had worked so well for such a long time.

The Schwanigers were initially quite leery of their American guest, doubly so as nobody in the hamlet had ever seen an American. Commencing with his arrival and for about a week thereafter, each evening following dinner Hans would bring him to Rickenhaslaw Castle. Once there, he'd confiscate his pants and boots then lock him in a room at the top of the castle tower about a hundred feet above the ground. He was the castle's sole occupant as it appeared to Gene the castle had been uninhabited for a long time.

Each morning Hans would return with his clothing and he and Gene would walk back to the farm. Conversation was always minimal, if any.

The Schwanigers were polite but not particularly outgoing. One bit of conversation Gene recalls concerned Hans' curiosity as to which state he was from. Gene told him: "Illinois." From the reaction, a mere shrug of his shoulders, Gene assumed Hans had no relatives living there.

The routine of locking Gene into the castle each night lasted about a week. Once the Schwanigers discovered he could play the piano, their attitude abruptly changed and they began to treat him as if he were a relative, albeit a very distant relative. They explained to him their son was a Luftwaffe fighter pilot stationed somewhere on the Eastern Front and was only a few years older than Gene. The two men were about the same size so they moved him into their son's room and instructed Gene to pack away his "rotten kleider" and wear their son's clothes, which were much more appropriate for working on a farm, and cleaner.

Having noticed that Gene's boots were seriously rotted, Hans provided him with a pair of Dutch wooden shoes—good both for working on the farm and as everyday footwear. He quickly learned to shuffle his feet, because if he walked normally the rigid tops of the shoes would jab into the instep of his ankles. He had previously noticed everyone wearing wooden shoes also wore thick socks and realized the socks tended to soften the harsh effect of wood-on-skin. The best he could manage was to double up on his socks, and shuffle. He also learned a hard and fast rule observed by everyone in the hamlet: to leave their dirty wooden shoes outside the front door lest they bring unsavory elements of the farm into their homes.

For the first time since his hospital stay Gene found himself sleeping in a genuine bed with a comfortable mattress and thick, feather-filled pillows. He certainly didn't miss the wire and straw bunks of Stalag VII-A. The resulting good sleep noticeably improved both his physical health and mental outlook.

Though there wasn't an overabundance of food, there was a great deal more to eat and it was, in Gene's words, "tremendously more flavorful and fresher" than the food he had eaten since his brief stay in the Nijmegen windmill. While there was more food available, he could only consume a small quantity at a time or he'd become sick to his stomach. He attempted to eat more often to compensate for his shrunken stomach and would carry bits of his most recent meal in his pockets to serve as snacks throughout the course of a work day.

Hans owned a short-wave radio and most evenings were spent sitting quietly and listening to music. Gene recalls feeling particularly homesick one night when Hans picked up a broadcast of big band music originating in San Francisco.

Hans possessed a John Deere tractor but lacked fuel to operate it, leaving Gene to till the land with a cow and an ox, harnessed to a single wooden yoke, pulling a single-share wooden plow. He milked the cows and discovered he was quick to pick up the various tasks he was asked to perform, never arousing any curiosity with his hosts as to his true background. He learned to make cheese and tend to the chickens as he became an adept and valuable assistant to the farmer, just as the German High Command likely intended. Gene much preferred working on a farm with no guards around him to life back at Moosburg. The Schwanigers didn't have any firearms and, apparently, nobody else in the enclave did either as Gene never saw one.

Over time Gene learned the farmers were basically sharecroppers indebted to Baron Rickenhaslaw's heirs for everything. Some of the families in the close-knit community had lived there since feudal times and little had changed over the centuries.

When the Baron's heirs had the odd job to be performed, they would hire only from within the hamlet to carry out the work. It was basically a self-sustaining society. The heirs also derived income by operating a small brewery from the cellar of the castle.

Hans was charged with operating the brewery and would make weekly excursions to personally deliver the beer to the various small pubs in the nearby hamlet. He utilized an oxen-drawn, V-shaped cart which could hold up to eight barrels of beer. Two barrels would be on the first row with three barrels on the second row. Two barrels comprised the third row and a single barrel sat on top. Hans was known to spend a little time at each pub having a beer or two with the pubmeisters and their patrons.

Eventually Hans decided he could trust Gene and put him to work in the brewery as often as three days a week. Thereafter Gene split his time between working on the farm and the brewery. He preferred the brewery.

At first Hans and Gene would deliver the Rickenhaslaw beer to the various taverns together. Gene recalls while the taverns were very small, they appeared to him to be a key part of the town's social fabric where men could freely gather and discuss various matters. The village itself was not much more than a collection of scattered houses, some doubling as businesses. It was a simple life and quite distanced from the actual conflict. A new section of the graveyard was the only indication the country was at war.

After a short time delivering the beer together, Hans decided Gene could handle the deliveries on his own and turned the chore over to him. He took full advantage of the situation and would consume an entire day delivering the barrels of beer and partaking with the locals, who called him "Oiygen." Invariably they always had a sandwich waiting for him. Despite taking an entire day to complete a morning's work, Hans never complained.

One morning Gene was working in one of Hans's farm fields, having been excused from his brewery duties for the day. It was rare to see any aircraft as the farm was significantly off the beaten path. However, he noticed a P-51 Mustang flying directly overhead. As he was following the plane's path the pilot suddenly dropped the external fuel tank directly into the field where Gene was working. Gene shook his fist at the pilot when the expended tank plunged into the ground not more than a hundred feet away from him.

The Germans were keenly aware there could be as much as 20 gallons of fuel remaining in the expended tank so Gene was not surprised when a staff car appeared, just minutes later, and retrieved it. The Germans never wasted an opportunity to obtain gasoline from any source imaginable.

On Sunday afternoons the entire town would gather in the modest central park situated within the castle walls and centered by an ornate gazebo. Gene was always invited to join the Schwaniger family and partake in the festivities. There would be a polka band complete with tuba, accordion, clarinet, and drum players. The townsfolk, dressed in traditional lederhosen, would dance. The food offerings included hearty sausages, bread, spicy mustard, sauerkraut, and of course, Rickenhaslaw beer—usually more beer than sausages. There were no young men to dance with the young ladies so Gene found himself a much-in-demand dance partner.

After some time passed Hans determined one of his bulls was approaching the end of his usefulness as a farm animal and he needed to slaughter it. The hide, meat, and blood would be most welcome. Though it was his bull Hans was obligated to obtain the local government's permission before he could proceed, so he made the requisite application. A couple of days later a Nazi Party representative appeared, slaughtered the bull, and took one half of the bull with him. Hans had no choice, though he was allowed to retain all of the blood from which he would make bloodwurst.

A couple of days later Gene and Hans were faced with unloading a wagon piled high with hay. Hans told him he'd take care of it and proceeded to make several unsuccessful attempts to lift himself onto the back of the wagon so he could climb to the top of the stacked hay and unload it.

His wife was standing nearby, hands on hips, watching him try and try again. Suddenly, unbeknownst to Hans and without saying a word, she walked up behind him. With her left hand she grabbed Hans by the back of the collar and with her right hand she gripped his bottom and in one quick motion flung him high onto the hay. He directed a few choice words toward her, tucked in his pants, and proceeded to unload the wagon without even once glancing at Gene. For Gene's part, he was able to keep from laughing and quickly walked around the side of the barn lest Hans's wife get some ideas about tossing him around as well.

He had been with the family a little more than a month when word came their son had been killed in action. The entire town, including the Baron's heirs, turned out for the funeral. It was late March 1945.

Easter came early that year, on the first of April. Mrs. Schwaniger staged an Easter egg hunt, with Gene as the sole participant. He couldn't remember the last time he had taken part in such an event and went along with it, especially as he did enjoy hard-boiled eggs and they were gentle on his stomach. Later the same day the Easter celebration at the castle proved to be a subdued event; there was a great deal of speculation the

Russian Army was coming toward Landshut and would soon over-run their little hamlet.

Stories of Russian atrocities had already been circulating and Gene wondered how they would treat him should they arrive and capture him, especially dressed as a civilian. He decided that should they appear he wouldn't rely solely on his POW dog tags and would immediately seek out his uniform to avoid possible execution. He always kept one eye on the horizon while working the farm as a precaution should the Russians actually arrive.

He didn't need to worry about the prospect of a Russian invasion for very long. A couple of days later the corporal from Stalag VII-A showed up with two other American POWs in tow. He was under orders to bring all three of the men back. Hans Schwaniger and his wife attempted to talk the corporal into giving Gene his rifle and letting him stay so he could, as an American, protect them in the event the Russians appeared. The corporal assured Hans and his wife the Russians were far to the north and east and not to be concerned. Gene found himself recalled to Stalag VII-A and dreading the prospect of returning to that nightmare.

CHAPTER EIGHTEEN

Escape!

Gene didn't know the two American prisoners and they were not Airborne. Regardless, the three of them greeted each other enthusiastically, shook hands, and exchanged names. The two men explained they'd been walking all day without eating and were of the opinion Gene was the last man the corporal was to retrieve. It was already mid-afternoon when the four men began the return journey to Stalag VII-A, on foot. There was no train service available at the time.

During the first night of the journey the corporal chose to encamp in a barn on the outskirts of what appeared to be a small town. The group bedded down in some haystacks after eating the meager meal the corporal had brought with him. Apparently he wasn't aware of the fact a military target existed in the town; the hub of important, intersecting railroads, it presented tempting targets to British and American bombers.

In the middle of the night air-raid sirens began sounding. There soon followed a full-on air bombardment, raining deadly and deafening explosions all around them. Fragments of debris battered the barn's roof. The entire structure shook violently with each concussion. Large and small pieces of shrapnel ripped through the wooden walls, placing all of them in peril.

Amid the confusion Gene and his two new friends ran off into a nearby woods, while the corporal, not thinking about his prisoners, dashed away to take cover elsewhere in the darkness.

The Swiss border was not terribly far away and Gene, accompanied by his two new pals, huddled together to discuss their situation. After a few minutes it was decided they'd try to reach Lake Constance where they planned to commandeer a boat and row to Switzerland. It sounded like a reasonable plan to Gene as long as they only traveled at night and stayed out of sight during daylight.

Based upon what he learned while living with the Schwanigers, he calculated it would be not more than a three- or four-day journey. He thought about mentioning the war couldn't last much longer and maybe they should wait things out but the thought of imminent freedom was too much to resist. He also shunted to the back of his mind the numerous times his guards had told him they shot escapees.

The clandestine group made good time the first night, with just enough moonlight to guide them. Gene recalled his old Boy Scout training and relied upon the North Star; his two companions were city boys and had no idea what direction they were going. He pointed them south and west, keeping the North Star behind his right shoulder.

The group was crossing a farm field when an explosion momentarily lit up the entire area. They immediately threw themselves to the ground and began looking around for the source of the blast when they noticed a series of utility poles running along the far edge of the meadow. A transformer had blown, which meant someone would soon be coming along to check it out.

They decided to remain where they were, clinging to the ground in the middle of a large, open field with the only cover provided by splotches of tall grass. They felt they were better off remaining prone and waiting things out.

Soon a half-track loaded with soldiers and some engineers arrived to fix the transformer. Once the soldiers left, they resumed their journey. Unfortunately, the delay had cost them nearly two hours of precious darkness. At the first sign of dawn they moved deep into a forest where they felt reasonably safe and spent the day, each of them taking a turn keeping watch. After sunset they continued their traveling, thirsty and hungry, the thought of freedom propelling them forward.

Around midnight they came upon a town. It presented them with a problem, as it lay directly between them and their ultimate objective, Lake Constance. Gene told his two fellow escapees they had no choice

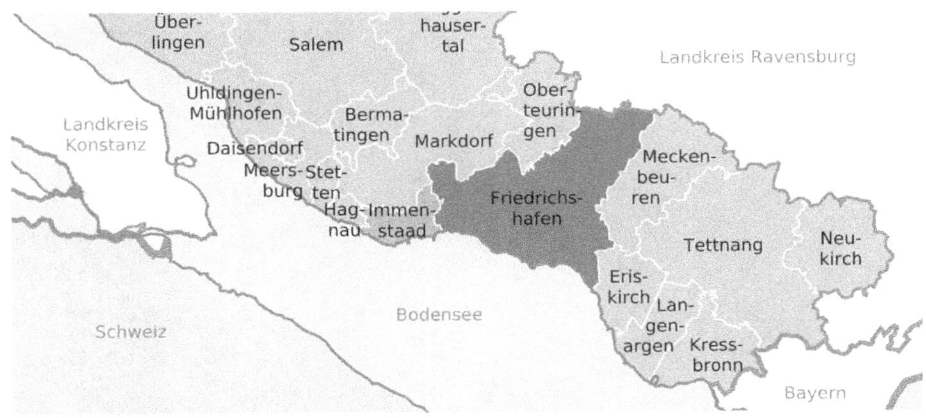

Friedrichshafen bordered Lake Constance. Switzerland was across the lake.

but to work their way around the settlement, even though it could cost them an additional day of travel. His two companions disagreed and wanted to, in their words, "sneak through" the town center as it appeared "quiet enough" to them.

Gene explained to them their proposed strategy of sneaking through the town "didn't work too well for me in Holland" and he would catch up with them on the other side. They separated and Gene veered left, safely into the forest, while the other two men, as discreetly as they could, made their way directly toward the town's center.

Gene was about halfway around the settlement when he heard gunshots originating from somewhere within the town. Quickening his pace, he arrived on the other side of the city about an hour or so before dawn. He settled in, hoping his friends would show up—in fact, he would never see them again. As daylight replaced night he decided to pull back into the woods, where he would spend a very nerve-wracking day. He needed to be on constant alert, for fear soldiers might be looking for him as a consequence of his friends' misguided venture the night prior.

CHAPTER NINETEEN

Recapture

Following sunset, Gene resumed his quest, trying hard to ignore the hunger pangs and making do with the occasional berry. While there was an abundance of mushrooms, a near-fatal experience eating wild mushrooms as a youth prevented him from sampling them again. As sunrise approached, he was shivering from the cold and desperately needed to find a place to hide out for the coming day. He'd been walking through a series of meadows and plowed-over farm fields. He knew he needed much better cover and intended it would be provided by a forest about 300 yards distant.

A heavy mist enshrouded the entire area, blurring the point at which the meadow merged into the forest. As he proceeded through the waist-high grass, he noticed a slightly raised road between him and his objective. He slowed his pace and cautiously approached the roadway when he spotted something. Instinctively, he dove head-first into the wet ground. His face was splattered by the dew clinging to the tall grass, causing him to vigorously wipe his eyes with the palms of his hands. He blinked a few times, then searched up and down the road.

He was startled when he spotted a lone German soldier about 60 or 70 feet away, out in the middle of nowhere, walking his post. Goosebumps ran up and down his spine. As the soldier slowly marched back and forth, Gene could clearly see his overcoat flapping in the faint breeze, making a sound like a bird taking flight.

He lay prone as he counted the German's measured paces: 30 steps toward him, then he'd turn around and take 30 steps in the opposite direction, the distinctive sound of his hob-nailed boots echoing in Gene's ears as he marched closer, turned around, and marched in the opposite direction. He was so close to the lone sentry he could hear the man cough.

With full daylight less than an hour away Gene decided he had little choice. Despite being unarmed and physically distressed he had no course of action other than make an attempt, in Gene's words, "to take him out." Time was running short; soon the sun would break over the tree-lined horizon and he'd be exposed and either captured or shot.

When the sentry turned around to march the opposite direction, Gene slowly and quietly rose, then quickly ran up behind him. He lifted his arms over his head, and just as he was about to leap upon the as yet unaware sentry, Gene froze. He found himself facing a large wooden post. There had never been a sentry!

The experience left him shaken as he quickly made his way toward the forest. He was certain there had been a guard. He had carefully observed him; he heard him cough and he counted the soldier's steps, yet it was all a very unsettling hallucination. Gene feared he was losing his sanity and whispered aloud: "I could get killed if I don't get a grip on myself." As he walked away he stopped to glance behind him. All he saw was the wooden post.

A short time later, having reached the forest and just as the sun was rising above the horizon, he detected a faint humming sound. He decided to check it out, slapping his cheeks a couple of times first to reassure himself it was not another figment of his imagination. He proceeded in the direction of the unidentified sound.

The entire forest was covered with a heavy dew, when he came upon an obstacle in the form of a 15-foot-deep ravine. As he began to carefully traverse the steep stone and loose gravel trail, he was startled at the sight of a thin wire running across the pathway ahead of him. His worn-out boots resisted his attempt to stop as they failed to grip the unstable surface and he found himself helplessly tumbling end-over-end until he came to a skidding halt at the bottom of the path.

He remained flat on his back, staring at what appeared to him to be a fuzzy spider web. He was out of breath, his head was spinning, and his arms and legs were outstretched as if he were making a snow-angel.

"There's something odd about it," he thought to himself as the rays of the sunlight began to illuminate what his eyes believed to be a spider web.

It took him a few moments to focus his eyes and for the spinning sensation to stop. That's when he realized the web was a single orange string and was anything but a spider web. As he stared at it the orange coloring turned out to be an illusion caused by a combination of the dew clinging to the "web" and the odd angle of the early morning sunlight.

Instinctively, he sensed something was very wrong. Remaining on his back he slid a couple of feet away, carefully got onto his knees, and inched up nearer to the web. Close examination confirmed it wasn't a web. The reality was he was staring at a copper wire strung about 4 feet above the ground. He carefully followed it a few feet further into the ravine to the base of a pine tree where it fed into the top of a green metal box.

He estimated the dimensions of the box to be approximately 9 or 10 inches high by 7 or 8 inches wide and at least 3 inches deep. At first glance he thought it was some manner of communications junction box. After staring at it a little longer, he came to the alarming conclusion it was an armed booby trap, the first one he'd ever seen. He found himself momentarily queasy when he realized he'd nearly fallen on top of the trip wire while wildly tumbling down the stone path. It was yet another perilously close brush with death and momentarily left him feeling, in his own words, "discombobulated."

Once he regained his composure he recognized the humming noise was still present, only louder. He followed the ravine a short distance until there was a sudden fall-off where he could look down on what he concluded to be a hydroelectric power plant that couldn't have been more than a couple hundred yards away. It was situated alongside a dam and the entire complex was heavily guarded. Gene experienced chills all over his body at the sight of the guards. Without hesitating, he slowly and quietly backed further into the gorge until he was safely out of sight.

After spending the day in the relative safety of the forest, he decided it was time to resume his journey. Based on his experience with the booby trap he nearly touched off, he determined the more prudent

A German booby trap bomb similar to the type Gene encountered. (Photograph courtesy of Andy at Arundel Militaria, United Kingdom)

course to follow would be one where he'd avoid pathways of any type on the assumption they could also be booby trapped, or even land-mined.

During the following day he stuck with his routine: traveling by night and hiding out in wooded areas during the day. It was approaching dawn when he noticed a lake and decided it must be Lake Constance, which he knew shared a border with Switzerland. By dead reckoning and the occasional road sign he figured the small city lying between him and freedom was probably Friedrichshafen. There were no "Welcome to Friedrichshafen" signs but he was pretty sure it was the only possibility.

As he investigated further he could clearly observe the snow-capped mountains of Switzerland. The first visible rays of sun were beginning to reflect off the calm surface waters of the lake, creating an appearance of peace and harmony. He had to shake his head a couple of times to be sure what he was looking at was genuine for he no longer completely trusted his own eyes.

He calculated whether he could reach the docks and the scores of unattended boats tied up there before the sun was fully risen. He didn't think it possible and his instincts were urging him to move deeper into the forest and wait for nightfall. Once it was dark he could make a night-crossing as he had planned all along.

His eyes, however, could plainly appreciate Switzerland's presence on the other side of the lake, and the yearning for freedom welling up inside of him proved impossible to ignore. Until then he had mostly made the right choices, keeping him alive to that point; now, however, he proceeded to make a potentially fatal decision, as he moved quickly toward the lake and the wooden docks. He imagined grabbing one of the boats and making the relatively short dash to the other side of the lake, and freedom. He had not considered that the boats would be padlocked. He also failed to take into consideration he'd be the only moving object on the lake and likely would gain some unwanted attention as a result.

With the sun peeking up over the horizon, Gene needed to decide whether to find a crowbar or something else he could use as leverage to break a padlock, or obey his instincts and retreat into the forest to await the cover of darkness. Hunger for both freedom and food drove him forward.

He made his second poor decision of the early morning and decided to seek out anything he might use to break open a padlock—a decision that brought him face-to-face with an armed German soldier accompanied by a leashed German Shepherd who began barking and pulling hard on the leash, anxious to be let loose at him. The soldier immediately pointed his rifle toward Gene's torso and beckoned for him to come over and face him.

It was obvious to him Gene was an escaped prisoner: he had not cut his hair, shaved or even washed his uniform since he jumped into Holland. He also sported the German prisoner-of-war dog tags around his neck and a German-mandated "KGF" prisoner-of-war patch, partially obscured by dried blood on his battle jacket. As Gene approached the sentry he saw that, though he was a young man, he sported a pair of battle decorations on his blouse, which Gene took to mean he was dealing with a Wehrmacht veteran. He quickly formulated a game plan to prevent him from being shot but his thoughts were interrupted by the German.

In broken English the German told him: "I am ordered to shoot any escaped prisoners!"

He didn't immediately shoot Gene, who noticed the German was staring at the bloodstains on his battle jacket. Gene decided to try to reason with him and answered in broken German: "If you were captured…" Shaken, Gene was at a temporary loss for words and blurted out: "I'm only doing my duty. Would you expect to be shot for doing your duty and attempting to escape?"

The German appeared to relax and replied in German: "Don't do it again! Don't you know the Russians are coming? Why would you escape with them coming? You might not be so lucky next time, you know!"

The soldier escorted Gene to the town jail where he locked him in a cell and left. Gene spent the next two days alone in the cell, hungry, thirsty, cold, and fearing he would be left to die as nobody seemed to care he was there. On the third day, after having nothing to eat for about six days, he discovered his captors apparently were aware of him, as the

The prisoner's name would appear on the opposite side of the tags. (Photo courtesy of Brian Jenkins, CC BY-SA 3.0, Wikimedia Commons)

heat came on and he was given a little breakfast and water. His mood dramatically improved as the prospect of starving to death no longer appeared to be the consequence of his failed escape attempt.

Later the same day Gene was released into the custody of a German corporal. The two of them walked to a nearby train station and boarded a civilian passenger train bound for München. The corporal directed Gene to sit next to the window while he took the aisle seat to make certain Gene wasn't going anywhere.

As they had been moving forward through the railcar he passed a number of, in Gene's words, "nifty uniformed" German ski patrol soldiers who stood out from the other soldiers on the train. They wore distinctive shoulder patches with a daisy in the center. The yellow flower, over a sky blue background, was outlined in white stitching. He noticed their "fancy caps" featured a skull in the front-center, though they lacked the skull and crossbones of the "SS." The image of the colorful shoulder patch remains embedded in his memory.

As he settled into his seat a beautiful young blonde woman dressed as if she were returning from a skiing holiday took the seat facing his. She began to strike up a conversation with Gene, who was probably not the first American with whom she had spoken; she proved to be quite fluent in English. As Gene replied, the corporal intervened and ordered him to *"Halt den Mund!"* Gene had heard the phrase plenty of times before and knew it meant for him to shut up.

The young woman took an immediate affront and gave the corporal a thorough dressing down, making it clear her father was a very important man and her uncle was the mayor, or some other manner of München VIP. She pretty much put the stunned corporal in his place. He meekly apologized to her and looked away, allowing her to resume her conversation with no further interruptions.

Gene learned she was 18 years old and returning to her family home in München after being away on a skiing holiday at Zugspitze Mountain. She expressed a keen awareness the war was nearing an end and was extremely fearful the Russians would reach München before the Americans. She wrote out her home address, handed it to Gene, and implored him to come and stay with her as soon as the war ended. The young lady was adamant her father would be happy to have him there and she'd certainly take "very, very good care" of him. She told Gene he could stay as long as he desired. Gene assured her he could protect her from the Russians, or anyone else, took the note with her address, and immediately memorized it. He told her she'd be his first stop as soon as the war ended. Appearing both relieved and happy she told him: "*Ich werde für dich warten!*"

Gene understood it to mean she'd be waiting for him. He smiled at her and tucked the address into his jacket pocket when the dreaded feeling of déjà vu again made itself known.

Though his bad ear was facing the window he realized he was listening to the distinctive engine of a P-51 Mustang. He glanced out the window and noticed the low-flying Mustang was proceeding in a zig-zag pattern, slowing his flight, as he was probably ascertaining whether the train was civilian or military. Gene gave the guard a very hard elbow directly into his ribcage and pointed toward the plane. Initially annoyed, he looked out the window following Gene's pointed finger. His eyes opened wide at the sight of the P-51. He abruptly stood and frantically pulled down on the emergency stop cord. Parcels went flying across the railcar as the train screeched to a halt and everyone began pouring out the doors and scattering in all directions.

The P-51 pilot, apparently aware he was about to target a civilian train, patiently flew in wide circles until he had satisfied himself everyone was out of the train. He dropped to treetop level and lined up the steam engine as he made the first of two runs at it. As bullets penetrated the engine housing, Gene, who lay prone along with everyone else, watched as miniature gushers of angry steam began shooting from the engine. He thought the venting steam "looked a bit like Old Faithful." On the second pass the pilot received the reward he was seeking: the engine exploded in an intense cloud of white and black smoke.

In the confusion Gene lost track of the girl. His guard pulled himself together and indicated they would proceed on foot the remainder of the way to München, following the railroad tracks. As they walked away Gene looked back and noticed there were no bodies on the ground. The pilot accomplished his objective with no loss of life.

After about an hour's walk they reached a bombed-out section of the railroad line. Sitting just beyond the damaged track was a passenger train waiting to pick everyone up and complete the trip into München. Gene mused that though the war may be nearing an end, the German communication system was still functioning well.

When they finally reached München, Gene was taken directly to a local police station where he was locked into a cell, by himself. The sparsely lit and basically empty jail cell proved to be a far cry from his accommodations back in the Rockford, Illinois police station. After a few hours he was joined by two Russian prisoners who nodded an acknowledgment to him as they took up quarters on the opposite side of the cell. A little while later a well-dressed French Army captain joined them. He was carrying a large suitcase plastered with travel posters and held together by a pair of ropes. Gene thought he looked to be a dead-ringer for the popular actor Errol Flynn and could certainly be no older than 35.

The dashing, rather tall Frenchman spoke fluent Russian and briefly engaged the two Russian prisoners in a conversation. He then turned to face Gene and, after first giving him a good looking-over, introduced himself as "Captain LaBorde." He proceeded to explain, in very good English, he was a medical doctor in the French Army. He told Gene shortly after the 1940 offensive broke out he was riding in the back of an ammo wagon on his way to serve as the division physician within the Maginot Line. A column of tanks was coming toward them, which they assumed were French, so the driver pulled over to the side of the road to let them pass. Unfortunately it proved to be a column of German tanks. Upon learning he was a medical doctor, a German colonel told him: "We can use you." The colonel politely ordered them to keep driving east, toward Germany. He did not need to travel very far before he found himself a prisoner of the Germans.

He went on to explain that as a French medical doctor the Germans allowed him a great deal of leeway. The Germans granted LaBorde the privilege of retaining his medical tools along with a suitcase of personal belongings. His captors didn't even confine him to a prison camp. He said he spent the war working as a surgeon in various military hospitals in Germany and, for a time, in Russia, where he picked up the language. The Germans would arrange for him to live in nearby private residences wherever he was stationed, be it Russia or elsewhere, allowing him the opportunity to further refine his German and Russian language skills.

LaBorde shrugged his shoulders and said he had no idea where the Germans were sending him this time and didn't care as long as it wasn't "to the east." Apparently realizing he'd been conducting a one-sided conversation, he asked Gene: "What is your destination?"

"I'm on my way back to Stalag VII-A, about 25 miles from here, near Moosburg."

"Ah, I understand. The Germans had me employed at a hospital here in München. You see, what I've been doing the last few months is slipping away from my assignment and boarding a train to take me as close to France as possible. I was caught each time, but I was also closer to home each time. It just happens they have caught me again." He then clapped his hands and exclaimed: "I imagine you probably have not eaten yet today! Are you hungry, Gene?"

"Are you kidding? The only restaurant around here was bombed out months ago and this place doesn't have room service."

LaBorde went to the cell door and called out to the German guard. After a brief conversation the guard left and returned a short while later holding a stack of firewood which he passed through the cell grates. In exchange, LaBorde handed him two cigarettes.

LaBorde proceeded to untie the ropes holding his beat-up suitcase together which popped open to reveal a rusty one-gallon pot, cabbage, carrots, potatoes, beets, and other vegetables. There was nary a pair of socks in the suitcase as it was filled with vegetables and eating utensils. He built a fire, filled the pot with water, added the vegetables, and set it atop a makeshift pot holder. The Russians looked on with envy but made no attempt to snatch any of the food for themselves. For his part, LaBorde didn't offer them any either.

The cell quickly filled with smoke as the sole window was up high and insufficient to clear the air, forcing Gene and LaBorde to sit on the floor, below the smoke layer. The Russians huddled in their corner, coughing from the smoke and ogling the food.

LaBorde withdrew a pair of dinner dishes from his suitcase and engaged in friendly conversation. As they consumed the makeshift stew, Gene found him easy to like and enjoyed their conversation very much. LaBorde explained to Gene it was his opinion the war could not last more than a few weeks at most; the Germans were in full retreat and were running out of places to hide. He wrote his Paris address on the back of a newspaper flyer, handed it to Gene, and expressed his intentions.

"Once the war is finished, come to my chateau in Paris and spend a week or two with me. I will show you around the city and we will have a good time; indeed, a very good time."

Gene accepted the paper with the address and shoved it into the same pocket holding the München address of the beautiful young skier. He replied: "I'll be there as soon as I can but I must make a stop in München first."

Early the next morning, two German soldiers came for Gene and escorted him back to Stalag VII-A, where he found conditions had deteriorated still further. He learned some of his friends had died of starvation while he was gone. He considered he may have been among the dead if he had not told the German interrogator at Stalag XII-A he had been a "*Bauer*" prior to the war.

CHAPTER TWENTY

Stalag VII-A, Again!

Gene spent the first few days of his return to VII-A in a *"Sonder"* barracks reserved for the retention of disobedient prisoners. Much to his surprise, it was actually a better living situation than elsewhere in the Stalag and he was provided an entire loaf of bread each day to himself. In addition, the cell, unlike the barracks, didn't "stink to high heaven." He was supposedly being punished, yet they were providing him more food than if he had been back in the American compound. As he would later say: "Go figure!"

Once he was released to the American barracks he immediately discovered food rationing at VII-A was worse than ever and a number of the men were no longer capable of walking without assistance. Russians continued to pour in and the meadow "gulag" was full of prisoners who were slowly starving to death. The moans and pleas emanating from the meadow underscored how dire the situation had become for many of the Russians.

By this time Gene had grown a long, lice-infested, auburn-colored beard. As with his beard, his lengthy hair and dirty uniform were also host to a hoard of lice constantly making their presence known through their crawling and biting. Without functioning bathing facilities available, virtually all of the prisoners were afflicted with lice and forced to live within the near-suffocating stench of the barracks. He was no different than the other prisoners as they all suffered from open sores over much of their bodies. The hospital offered no relief as it was barren of supplies. If a prisoner were to suffer a severe cut, there weren't any bandages; the doctor instead relied upon paper to wrap the wound. Then one day something very out of the ordinary happened.

The Germans forced the American POWs to completely disrobe, ostensibly for the purpose of delousing their uniforms. The Germans had never done so in the past, and while waiting for their clothing to be deloused the Americans were marched into showers for the first time ever. A large number of Mongolian families—men, women and children—joined them in the showers, creating what Gene described as "a very weird scene." He wondered what the Germans were up to.

To his relief the Germans returned their unwashed, but deloused, clothing. Later in the day they resumed life as it had been before as if nothing had transpired. Gene thought the entire event to have been very strange. The reason for the delousing and shower was never brought to light, though one guard did explain the presence of the Mongolians. They were Germany's allies in the fight against Russia and when they were in danger of being over-run by the advancing Russians, the German Army shipped them into Germany for their own protection. The Mongolians' train had been parked on the Moosburg siding for the day and the Germans decided to treat them to showers.

Later the same day one of the guards with whom Gene had become friendly told him he'd had himself a 14-day leave. He used the occasion to travel home to Berlin where he could not locate his house amongst the rubble. Nor could he make contact with any of his family or friends. He cut short his leave and returned early as he refused to accept the fact his home, family, and friends were gone. He harbored no desire to continue his search for them lest he discover they had, in fact, all been killed. He told Gene he'd rather believe they were safe somewhere in the countryside.

He asked Gene where he had been and Gene told him he'd been assigned to work on a farm out toward Landshut. Upon hearing the name of the town the guard brightened up and asked if it had also been bombed. He was genuinely happy to learn Landshut had not yet been bombed, as he had a distant relative living there.

The guard went on to explain he had been at Stalingrad and described how the Russians would charge directly into their tanks and machine-gun fire by the hundreds, only to be mowed down en masse. He said in one day alone he had to replace the barrel of his machine gun eight times; he could barely fire fast enough to keep "the crazy Russians" at bay. To his amazement the Russians would continue their charges the next day. He said they couldn't kill them fast enough and there always seemed to be more of them in reserve. He confided it had been very demoralizing to be killing so many of them and yet see no improvement in the tactical situation. He confessed to Gene he would probably always be haunted by the memories of never-ending Russian hordes charging toward him.

His life was saved from the fate of the rest of his comrades in the German Sixth Army when he was seriously wounded and placed onto a plane only days before the last airport was overrun by the Russians. It took almost a year for him to recover from his wounds, after which he was assigned to the Stalag. He had hoped to be discharged and allowed to go home but was informed even the most severely wounded were rarely discharged from service. Gene thought to himself he'd be having his own nightmares, thanks to the Germans, and didn't feel much compassion for his captor.

Though the town of Moosburg didn't present much in the way of military targets, the British would, from time to time, bomb in the vicinity of the town. Sometimes they knocked out the water supply to the prison camp or the latrines. On at least one occasion the bombing victims were a few cows grazing in a field alongside the camp, the remains of which modestly supplemented the following days' meals. On another occasion a horse was killed and was added to their "menu." Gene could hardly notice the difference, though he did seem to discern a slight "sweetness" to the little bits of horsemeat that made it into his pan.

The morning of April 13, 1945, all the guards were very excited. They were talking and joking, leading Gene to think the Allies just took another turn for the worse in the war. He motioned to the same guard with whom he conversed the day before and asked him what was going on. With a broad grin on his face he replied: "Rozenfelt dead, you will quit the war now."

"Rozenfelt?" Gene asked.

"*Ja, ja,* he died yesterday. You know, Rozenfelt, your leader."

"Oh, you mean President Roosevelt is dead." Gene replied. "Sorry, but that's not how a democracy works. You see, we have a vice-president who immediately takes his place and everything goes on as it was."

The German was clearly disappointed. He shook his head and slowly walked away, his bubble of elation totally flattened.

Later the same day the air-raid sirens sounded as a large formation of American bombers appeared overhead on their return trip west. Watching from one of the windows in his barracks, Gene observed two Russian prisoners who failed to return to their barracks. They remained outside in blatant disregard of the air-raid rules as they pointed toward the bombers and laughed at the guards who were less than entertained by their antics. He had witnessed such a scene back at Stalag XII-A and immediately became alarmed.

One of the guards in particular was threatening the two Russians who, with not much to lose, were having a good laugh at his expense. He pointed his rifle at them but they refused to return to their barracks until another guard appeared with a German Shepherd. He unleashed the dog, which immediately charged directly at the two Russians. The Russians quickly sprinted into their barracks with the dog right on their heels ready to pounce, the barracks door slamming shut just after the dog entered. Gene and his fellow prisoners laughed at the sound of all hell breaking loose inside the Russian barracks. They could only imagine the havoc created by the raging dog.

Once the air raid was over the German who had unleashed the dog returned, holding the leash in his hand and calling out the dog's name. The dog did not respond. He started to walk in the direction of the barracks when he suddenly stopped in his tracks, his mouth popping wide open. He was staring at his dog's hide hanging across the barbed-wire fencing just outside one of the barrack's windows. The Russians had eaten his dog, raw.

He quickly left and returned a few minutes later with an additional dozen soldiers. They forced their way into the barracks and again there was a great deal of commotion. Eventually the guards reappeared, dragging three Russian prisoners with them. They threw them onto the ground and shot them dead. A few moments earlier Gene and his pals had been laughing at the goings-on and, just like that, the laughter disappeared as quickly as it had begun. Gene learned a German Shepherd was worth the lives of three Russians.

The same afternoon yet another column of Russian prisoners was ushered in and divided into two groups as usual. Perhaps due to a possible ammunition shortage, the Germans marched the group failing the "physical exams" into the meadow "gulag" to join their comrades in a slow death. It would be at least another week before all the Russians in the "gulag" would die as the weather had begun to moderate.

Early the following evening it was raining hard—a cold, penetrating rain that forced Gene to remain in the barracks. He passed the time observing a scraggly looking pregnant black cat in search of food. He watched it wind its way among the barbed-wire fencing, coming and going as it pleased.

Gene pointed to the cat and mentioned to a friend how the cat had it so much better than they did as it could do as it wanted, coming and going as it desired. The cat wandered over to their open door, where he and some of his friends petted and stroked it. Not finding any food the cat disappeared into the compound.

All the prisoners spent as much time outside of the barracks as possible. They had only showered on the one occasion, the result being the barracks smelled worse than anything Gene had ever experienced in his life. The only daylight hours they would spend in the barracks occurred during air raids and the occasions when the weather was even more foul than the barracks.

The main topic of conversation was always food. Men would describe their favorite restaurants or their mom's wonderful cooking and perhaps speculate about how they intended to open a bar or restaurant after the war. With hunger and the accompanying listlessness eating away at them, topics such as escaping or war news were low on the conversation priority list. After the subject of food, joke telling was a popular pastime, an area in which Gene was an expert. Talking about females was last on the conversational totem pole as most men grew melancholy when the discussion turned to females.

Mail call was, at best, an irregular event. Though most of the men hardly ever received any mail there was one mail call when Gene received 15 letters, some of them with the edges of the envelopes partially burned. He was the only recipient of mail in his barracks that particular day.

Looking at the stack of mail, he could only imagine what the envelopes went through to reach him. All 15 letters were from Betty, and after reading the first five or six letters, he realized a crowd was gathered around him, all attempting to read over his shoulder. He decided to pass a few letters out, after first reading them himself, to anyone who cared to read one, which was just about everybody. It didn't matter they were reading a letter written for someone else. Each man appeared to imagine he was the intended recipient and thoroughly enjoyed the fantasy. As for Betty, Gene decided he'd deal with that situation when he returned home. He was never much for letter writing, but did include notes to Betty in the handful of letters he sent to his parents.

A couple of days following the black cat incident the weather cleared. Gene was milling around the compound and paused to observe the morning routine at the Russian compound as all the prisoners were lined up for the daily "head count." Once the count was completed the Russians dispersed throughout their compound.

A German officer was slowly walking away when Gene noticed him suddenly stop, pause, turn around, and approach three Russian prisoners who were still standing in line for the head count. They remained at attention, standing shoulder-to-shoulder. The officer was staring at the prisoner in the middle who appeared to be unusually stiff. The officer gestured with his arms to indicate the three men were to spread apart. As they did so the prisoner in the middle fell to the ground, rigid as a brick, having been dead for some unknown period of time. The officer screamed a few obscenities at the men who had propped up their deceased comrade, apparently upset they had been allocating one man too many for the daily rations.

Later the same day Gene was sketching a pair of P-51 Mustangs as they took turns buzzing the compound when a German "SS" captain approached him and confiscated his two volumes of sketches. The collection of sketches covered his entire period of confinement and he had spent countless hours creating them and countless more looking at them. Just like that, they were gone and there was nothing he could do about it as the captain carried a machine gun and Gene was nothing more than a living skeleton. Today, Gene muses, those two volumes of sketches may possibly be stored in a trunk, buried in an attic somewhere in Germany.

Shortly after losing his sketchbooks a British sergeant-pilot wandered over. Gene doesn't recall what he was doing in the American barracks, but he does remember the conversation. The Brit explained to him he had been captured on September 3, 1939. The pilot was extremely bitter for he was certain his commanding officer knew war was about to be declared. Nonetheless, he was dispatched on a photographic scouting mission over a Luftwaffe airfield in Germany.

He soon found himself with Messerschmitt 109s on either side of his unarmed reconnaissance plane. The Luftwaffe fighter pilots indicated he needed to immediately land at the airfield he had been photographing. Once on the ground he was advised the two countries were formally at war and he was taken prisoner, possibly the first British prisoner of World War II. He was especially miffed, because the Royal Air Force ceased paying him the moment he had been captured. Gene didn't know how to respond and after few moments of silence the pilot, apparently having said his piece, moved on.

Gene recalls it was a Sunday morning and they were told they'd be clearing bomb damage in München proper since the British had bombed the city the night prior. As they began to march across the bridge over the Isar River he noticed there was a dense haze draped over the city, the rising sun no more than a weak orange blot hiding behind the blueish-gray haze. The air was cold and damp, sending goosebumps up and down his arms and legs. A series of telephone poles had collapsed inwards, toward each other, the power lines drooping onto the street as if the poles had grown tired of supporting them. Glistening black ravens perched atop the bent poles as if they were inspecting the damage. Gene thought he was walking into a scene from Dante's *Inferno*, but it was München, late April 1945.

He paused to glance behind him. The large glass dome situated above the center of the München railway station had been shattered by a bombing raid, leaving bare metal girders, some of them twisted into odd shapes, as the only evidence of its past magnificence. Still hanging from a steel cable stretched across the base of the dome was an enormous Nazi flag. The irony was not lost on him.

CHAPTER TWENTY-ONE

Liberation

During the night of April 28, 1945, a substantial volume of traffic traveled on the road outside the Stalag, with trucks, motorcycles, tracked vehicles, marching soldiers, and horses all audible. The scuttlebutt went one of two ways: either the Germans were building up for another counterattack or they had dug in and were intent on making a stand at Moosburg. Gene hoped there was a third option and the Germans were actually retreating.

Prisoners in one of the other American barracks had been sneaking in radio parts from their work excursions in München and had constructed a working receiver. They painted a map of the European Theater on a wall of their barracks and were following the Allies' progress with large arrows. The guards assumed they were gaining their information in München and never discovered the radio; the problem for the American POWs was their radio intercepts revealed nothing of the goings-on near Moosburg.

When dawn broke it was obvious the majority of the approximately 2,000 guards had abandoned the camp, though the gates remained locked. A skeleton crew of approximately 200 guards remained to keep watch over 110,000 prisoners of war. Gene and his fellow prisoners discussed taking control of the camp when someone said he had reliable information to the effect Patton's tanks were on the outskirts of town. They decided it was worth waiting a few more hours rather than risk a number of them being killed.

Despite the two incidences when P-51s had flown over the camp, the Allies were as yet unaware of the existence of Stalag VII-A. Sometime on the afternoon of April 28, 1945, a group of four envoys, proceeding in a staff car flying a white flag, made contact with the lead elements of Patton's army. The envoys included two senior German officers and the senior British and American officers from the Stalag who were ostensibly brought along to testify as to the existence of the Stalag. The Germans were seeking an agreement with the Americans to turn the general area around Moosburg and Stalag VII-A into a sort of a neutral zone until the prisoners-of-war could be safely removed by the Allies.

The American general Daniel Gentry realized it was a ploy to allow enough time for elements of the 17th SS Panzergrenadier and 719th Infantry Division and an assortment of German army and mechanized units to cross the nearby Isar River. He refused the German proposal and continued to plan an assault on the town, as previously scheduled, for the following morning.

The discovery of the sprawling prison camp caused Gentry to modify the attack plan and refrain from the employment of an extended artillery barrage, as previously planned. If the Germans had not made contact with the Americans, Stalag VII-A may well have been subjected to a heavy artillery barrage as part of the assault on Moosburg. Without knowing it, Gene had again escaped death at the hands of the Allies.

Morale was high as the prospect of freedom proved contagious. One of the men, a barber by trade, was offering haircuts in exchange for cigarettes. He had a long line of customers, each anxious to look good for General Patton's men. There was even scuttlebutt that Patton intended to inspect the camp himself, notching up the level of anticipation.

As for Gene—his hair long and scraggly, his beard unkempt, and the blood from the machine-gunned prisoner he carried to the hospital in Stalag XII-A still splattered across the front of his battle jacket and trousers—by now he was far too skinny for his 6-foot 4-inch frame. But he didn't "give a hoot," as freedom was at hand. He momentarily recalled the sign at Camp Grant extolling: "Look your best as appearance is important" and laughed out loud at the memory. He said to himself: "Patton couldn't do anything more to me than the Germans had already done."

At 0830 hours on April 29, 1944, General George S. Patton's Sherman tanks began an assault on Moosburg. Bullets whizzed through the camp, forcing everyone to lie flat while the battle ensued. In about an hour it went completely silent.

Half an hour later Gene could hear tanks coming up the road, but this time they weren't Tigers. Three Sherman tanks slowly came around the corner of the old cheese factory. When they approached the main gate they were greeted by gunfire from the guard tower. One of the tank commanders returned fire with his .50-caliber machine gun, just about cutting in half the camp commandant, "SS" Colonel Hoffman. Hoffman had taken up a guard tower position and had been firing at them with a much lighter, and less effective, MG 42 machine gun. Apparently he decided he'd rather die than surrender. Having eliminated the only resistance, the lead tank blew open the gate and all three tanks rolled into the middle of the camp where they came to a halt and were immediately swarmed by thousands of elated prisoners.

In a few minutes the camp went from pandemonium to complete quiet at the sight of the Nazi flag coming down and Old Glory running up the flagpole. Just about everyone was crying for joy. For Gene, it was as if a tremendous weight had been lifted from his shoulders. In that moment the constant fear which had been his steady companion for eight months, continuously eating away at his stomach lining and clawing at his nerves, was gone. He was back in control of his life—a feeling so great that to this day he can't find the words to adequately describe it.

Word quickly spread of General Patton's intention to visit the camp the next day. For Gene it was time to enjoy the moment and get his hands on some chocolate. He spent the early part of the afternoon absorbing the sun, eating chocolate, and learning to appreciate cigars. Third Army tank crews brought vast quantities of chocolate, rations, cigarettes, and cigars to liberally distribute to the veterans of Stalag VII-A. As he leaned against an outside wall of his bunkhouse, his back against the railing, he "considered the possibilities."

A friend of his he knew to be Jewish, Ike Enloe, stopped to chat. It was the first time he learned that "Ike Enloe" was a name he borrowed when he switched dog tags with a deceased soldier in order to save his own life. Gene considered it to have been a smart move and no doubt did keep him from joining the men who were told they'd be back shortly, never to return. As "Ike" wandered off he thought about how elated his family would be when they learned he was still alive.

He decided to walk over to Moosburg, determined to explore "the possibilities." He didn't get far when a British sentry challenged him: "Where do you think you're going, Yank?" The unarmed sentry attempted to sound intimidating as his back stiffened. However, it was Gene's opinion the young Brit didn't know what real intimidation was. He appeared to be nothing more than a novice and besides, Gene reasoned, who put the British in charge of the camp?

"Right now I'm going into Moosburg and from there I thought I'd like to take in Paris," replied Gene, in a matter-of-fact manner.

The sentry placed himself between Gene and Moosburg and responded: "No you aren't, Yank. We're flying the lot of you out of here and back to sunny England tomorrow in our Dakotas."

"Listen, I've been to England but I haven't been to Paris and don't know if I'll ever get the chance again, so shoot me! Oh, and when you say, 'our Dakotas,' are you referring to the great American C-47 Skytrain aircraft, the best air transport in the world?"

A bit taken aback and suddenly intimidated himself, the sentry quickly moved to the side but not before getting off a final warning: "I'll have to report you, Yank!"

Gene paused, turned around to face him, and said: "You do that Tommy, and make damn sure it's a good one!"

The sentry shook his head, giving up the effort, and resumed his post as Gene continued into Moosburg, this time not as a prisoner but as a conqueror.

He acquired a bucketful of white wine, courtesy of some locals, sat down on a large, flat rock alongside the main road, and made himself comfortable watching a procession of American Sherman tanks, Jeeps, and supply trucks. Since he had nothing better to do he decided he'd camp out there and watch the parade.

As the tanks rolled along the street the tank crews would toss him cigars, cigarettes, K-rations, and chocolate bars. At one point a Sherman tank slowed to a stop. One of the tankers jumped out and cut loose a couple boxes of what were called, "10–1 rations." He cut the moderately heavy boxes loose one at a time and dropped them next to Gene. The tanker smiled, waved, climbed back atop the Sherman, and drove away.

The 10–1 ration carton was a veritable Pandora's box of excellent trading commodities, including canned butter-substitute spread, water-soluble instant coffee, pudding, meat in the form of either spam or bacon, jam, evaporated milk, vegetables, biscuits, cereal, beverages, candy, gum, salt, and sugar. It also included cigarettes, matches, a can opener, toilet paper, soap, towels, and water-purification tablets. To Gene the 10–1 was purely for bartering; he yearned for fresh food, not the canned and boxed stuff the passing tankers were tossing his way. His stomach was so shrunken he couldn't eat very much at one sitting so he determined, from then forward, he would eat only what he liked and as often as possible.

He lit a cigar, balanced his bucket of sweet, white wine on his lap, and acknowledged the occasional cheers directed at him by the passing tankers. It wasn't long before he began to feel a bit of a buzz from the wine. It was a beautiful day so he made himself a comfortable perch using a blanket a passing trucker had tossed to him. He couldn't imagine a better way to spend the afternoon. Besides, there was no reason to hurry and he was no longer, in his words, "under the gun."

As time passed and he became more comfortable, Gene began to notice the occasional small group of former Russian prisoners moving through the backyards of the homes across the street from him. It was probably inevitable one of the roving bands of former Russian POWs would happen upon an unaccompanied female.

When he heard screams coming from behind one of the houses he noticed some Russians standing in what to him looked to be a semicircle. When he realized they were raping a woman he tried to stand. Between his seriously depleted physical condition, the sun, and the wine, especially the wine, he realized he was in no condition to effect a rescue.

His attempts to draw the attention of passing tankers and trucks resulted in no more than an occasional nod. Eventually he saw a woman run into a nearby house and the Russians disappeared. It would not be the last time he'd witness Russians on the loose. The unarmed British sentries surrounding VII-A were apparently having no luck preventing the Russians from leaving the Stalag.

As the afternoon progressed and the road traffic died down, Gene was considering where to spend the night when he thought he heard someone calling his name from up the road. He looked in the direction of the voice and noticed a soldier not more than a couple hundred feet away, vigorously waving his right arm in the air as if trying to gain his interest. Gene didn't pay much consideration to him as he was very much enjoying an afternoon of wine, sun, freedom, and besides, he didn't recognize him. The soldier was running directly at him, his helmet bobbing up and down, but was failing to elicit a response despite constantly calling out "Mr. Metcalfe! Mr. Metcalfe!"

The soldier, a private, ran up and placed himself directly between Gene and the road when he said: "Are you from Illinois?"

"Yep," dead-panned Gene.

"Are you from DeKalb, Illinois?" the private asked.

"Yep," responded Gene, this time with a little more interest in his voice.

"Mr. Metcalfe—it's me, Billy Carey, don't you remember?" Billy repeated himself a couple of times as Gene stared at him, clearly not remembering. In frustration Billy dropped his rifle and shook Gene by the shoulders as if trying to wake him up.

"You came to my science class at DeKalb High and talked about the paratroops." Billy stopped shaking him when Gene's expression indicated a flicker of recognition.

"Well, right after your talk I decided to enlist, so here I am, just like I said. Mr. Metcalfe, don't you remember I said I'd see you in Germany?" Billy's voice conveyed more than a little hint of hurt feelings.

Gene smiled, slowly staggered up, and heartily shook Billy's hand.

"Damn Billy, I almost forgot. I know you said you'd meet me over here but I didn't believe it. You've got no idea what I've been through since then." He motioned to his hair and uniform. "Hard to believe you recognize me." He paused a moment, then asked: "What the hell are you doing here?"

"I'm a runner for Division HQ and I'm searching for a black platoon that's supposed to be somewhere around here, maybe even on the other side of the front lines. I need to deliver them an important message. They lost contact with us a couple of days ago." He paused to get his breath.

"Their last position was somewhere thataway." Billy pointed toward the horizon, further into Germany, exactly the opposite direction Gene intended to travel.

"Well, it's going to be dark soon Billy, and of all the units that came past here today, I've got to say, I didn't see any Black platoons, so they must be a heck of a piece up the road." Gene looked at the western horizon and noted the sun couldn't be more than an hour away from setting.

"It's going to be dark soon, I haven't eaten dinner, and I'm guessing you haven't either. I suggest we bed down for the night and I'll help you in the morning. How's that sound to you?"

"I guess that'd be swell, Mr. Metcalfe. I'm definitely hungry, but I have no idea where I'm going to sleep tonight."

"I've already figured that out." Gene turned and pointed to the meticulously maintained house behind him. It reminded him of an English Tudor and had a long, curvy, stone walkway leading from the road to the red-painted front door. "We're going to stay here."

"Do you know who lives there? Billy asked.

"I have no idea Billy. You have the M-1 and I have all these supplies," Gene pointed to the supplies littered all around him, "so I don't think it's going to be a problem. Grab everything you can, especially the 10–1, and follow me. Whatever you do don't leave any cigars or cigarettes behind."

Gene, his arms full of supplies, walked to the front door where Billy joined him, standing a little to his right. Billy put the supplies down and unslung his rifle as Gene knocked on the door. Billy was taking no chances there might be an unfriendly reception ahead and backed away a step or two for a more strategic angle.

The door partially opened, revealing an older couple. They were so terrified the wife was literally shaking. Gene smiled and in a gentle voice told them: "*Wir sind zum essen und bleiben sie die nacht.*" Apparently Gene's German was good enough to convey his intentions to have dinner and stay the night. They didn't argue and fully opened the door, allowing the two Americans to enter.

Gene and Billy proceeded to the kitchen where they filled the table with their foodstuffs. Gene took the rifle and advised Billy he'd check upstairs and the basement and suggested Billy "keep an eye on them."

Before leaving, he told the woman to "*Beginnen essen,*" which he intended to mean "start making dinner." As he walked toward the stairwell leading to the second story he could hear her quietly exclaiming her delight as she began to open the packages, bringing a smile to his face.

His search of the upstairs indicated there was probably someone else living in the home, not just the old couple. Gene was on double alert as he made his way down into the stone-floored basement. As he reached the bottom of the stairs he was confronted by three large barrels neatly lined up in the center of the short-ceilinged, dark, dank room lit by a single lightbulb.

The tops of the barrels were hinged in the center, allowing the homeowner to open only one half of the lid, or the entire lid. He opened the first barrel to find it was full to the brim with sauerkraut. The second barrel was similarly filled with sauerkraut. When he opened the lid to the third barrel he took a short step backwards, momentarily startled at the sight of a head-full of blonde hair tied into a pair of braids.

He reached in and discovered the couple's daughter, who would later explain she was 17 years old and was hiding in case the Russians came. In a friendly voice Gene said: "*Ich wird sie nicht,*" which he hoped meant, "I won't hurt you." He understood her fear.

Apparently his German was close enough as she stood and he helped her out of the barrel before escorting her to the kitchen. As well as he could, he proceeded to explain to his three German hosts they were in no danger from them. He cautioned them should the Russians ever appear they'd need a better hiding place for both the man's daughter and his wife.

While the wife and daughter put together dinner, Gene, Billy, and the husband went into the living room where they opened a few bottles of wine. Gene spied a beautiful Steinway grand piano and resisted the urge to sit down and play. He pulled out some cigars and the three men lit up, sat back, and enjoyed them.

When dinner was ready the wife placed it on the dining room table and left to join her husband and daughter in the living room. After some coaxing, Gene and Billy were able to convince the family they were invited to join them. During the dinner conversation Gene learned the husband was a music professor at a nearby college.

After dinner everyone retired to the living room. Before settling into one of their cozy armchairs Gene prevailed upon his guests for the use of a shower as he anticipated sleeping in a clean bed for the first time in "too long." Unfortunately, he had no choice other than to put his ragged, dirty uniform back on. After Gene joined everyone in the living room the professor opened a cabinet and produced a large, intricately carved gold pocket watch, which he placed on top of the Steinway. He set the watch to serve as a timer and proceeded to beautifully play the "Minute Waltz," in exactly one minute.

Gene picked up the watch, looked it over, and returned it to the owner, advising him never to pull it out in front of strangers, especially in these times. The professor shook his head in understanding. While Gene wanted to play the piano a bit himself, it proved impossible to wrangle it from the music professor, who played a nearly nonstop stream of songs until everyone was ready to retire for the night.

Gene experienced his best and most peaceful night's sleep in at least eight months and awoke to the smell of breakfast being cooked. The aroma of fresh eggs on a skillet brought a smile to his face. Following breakfast they sat around for a little while, engaging in conversation heavily supplemented with sign language. The family didn't want them to leave as they obviously felt safe with Gene and Billy present. Gene did his best to assure them as long as the Russians don't show up in force, and with Patton's army between them and the main Russian forces, they'd be okay. They tried hard to persuade Gene to stay with them for a few days. He explained to them he and Billy had an important military message to deliver and they had to leave.

The husband presented Billy with a beautiful pocket-watch as a present and demonstrated how it would play the "Minute Waltz." Billy shook his hand in gratitude and turned to leave, but not before the mother presented Gene with a beautiful, intricately adorned silver beer stein. He opened the lid and discovered she had packed it full of eggs, each egg carefully wrapped in paper. Gene attempted to reject the gift. She told him, as close as Gene recollects: "There will probably be people coming here after you who will not be so friendly and *they* will take it away from us so please accept it." Gene realized she was likely correct and relented.

Gene and Billy repeated their good-byes, but before they could depart their host insisted Gene pen a letter stating he had been well treated and these are good people. Gene knew such a letter from him would carry no weight so he signed it as: "Colonel Roy Lindquist, 82nd Airborne, 508th Paratroop Infantry Regiment."

As they exited the front door some passing tankers yelled out to them: "With that fucking Hitler dead the war's just about done!" Gene hadn't yet heard the news of Hitler's death in Berlin. He wondered what his German captors who had thought America would quit the war when "Rozenfelt" died must be thinking now. Distant cannon fire confirmed the war was not yet over.

Not interested in searching for the lost platoon on foot, Gene investigated a next-door neighbor's garage where he discovered an Opel convertible, sitting up on blocks. Gene told Billy to get some 5-gallon gas cans from the passing trucks and tanks. In a few minutes he returned juggling three 5-gallon jerry cans of gasoline.

"Gene, we don't have a key so how're we going to start it?"

"Don't worry Billy, I know how to start it. Just go get that air pump on the wall over there and start pumping up the tires." Gene smiled.

Gene opened the hood, poured a little gas into the carburetor, and proceeded to fill the gas tank. Before continuing he paused long enough to tell Billy once he was finished pumping up the tires to go fetch another couple cans of gas and put all of them into the back seat. While Billy went in search of more gasoline, Gene opened the driver's door, leaned beneath the steering wheel column, and located the requisite wire leads for hot wiring the car. He breathed a sigh of relief when he discovered the battery was not dead. After a couple of attempts the engine fired up.

Billy arrived with two more gas cans and exclaimed: "How'd you do that?"

"A little gas in the carb, a quick hot wire, and now we don't have to walk."

Gene stood back and looked at the car, frowning. Billy noticed and asked what he was worried about. Gene commented the car might be mistaken from the air as being an open-air German staff car. He looked around the barn and pointed to a large piece of orange-dyed canvas.

"Grab that canvas Billy."

The two men proceeded to tie the canvas to the rear bumper and stretched it over the top of the car, securing the leading edge to the front bumper. Billy cut a hole for the windshield and extended the opening just enough so they could sit in the two front seats. Gene took a step back and admired their ingenuity.

"No fighter's going to mistake this for a German staff car!"

As they pulled out of the garage in the modified convertible the car's owner rushed out of the house, shouting something Gene didn't understand. Gene called back to him: "*Erhalten sie Wagen en München,*" which Gene hoped would translate to: "You can pick up your car in München."

The man apparently understood and half-heartedly waved them goodbye.

They pulled onto the dirt road and pointed themselves east. In a few minutes they discovered a large firehouse on the edge of town and pulled into the main garage to check it out. There was nobody present. There were, however, about two dozen highly ornate firemen's swords with engraved blades housed in fancy sheaths hanging on the wall. There

A 1930s-era Opel convertible, possibly the model Gene and Billy "borrowed."

were large Nazi insignias in black, outlined in red, embedded between the ornate handle and the engraved blade. Gene immediately realized these could prove useful as trade material.

"Billy, stuff those swords into the backseat, they'll come in handy!"

Billy didn't question him, and once the swords were tucked away they continued to follow the road, leaving Moosburg behind them.

For the first half an hour or so they were frequently pulling over to the side of the road to allow faster moving tanks and trucks to pass them. As the morning wore on traffic thinned out considerably and eventually they were the lone vehicle on the road. Gene noticed a Sherman tank parked off to the right, just ahead of them, and pulled up behind it. He and Billy left the car and walked to the front of the tank. The tank commander, a sergeant with dark circles under his bloodshot eyes and perhaps a week's worth of stubble on his face, was leaning on the .50-caliber machine gun mounted on top of the turret.

"Say, how's it going, are you okay?" Gene asked with Billy, rifle slung on his shoulder, standing alongside him.

The sergeant looked down at them and in a monotone voice replied: "We're beat to hell and haven't slept in three days. That bastard Patton just keeps us goin' nonstop." He paused and sighed. "I'm just giving the tank a chance to cool off."

While Gene continued the conversation, he barely noticed three Jeeps race past them. The Jeeps slowed down about a tenth of a mile beyond and made a U-turn. Gene began to pay attention to them as they were barreling in his direction at full speed, throwing up a large cloud of dust behind them.

As the Jeeps approached he noticed four large stars on the second Jeep where a license plate would be located and flags flying on each fender, also bearing four stars each. The Jeeps featured a .30-caliber machine gun mounted between the front and second row seats. As they skidded to a halt a colonel sitting in the front passenger seat of the first Jeep called out to the tank sergeant: "What the hell are you doing here soldier—are you out of gas?"

He impatiently awaited an answer as the sergeant was slow to acknowledge him. Leaning a little more heavily onto his .50-caliber, his hand not far from the trigger, the sergeant responded: "No Sir, we're just damned tuckered out." His response was devoid of emotion and his eyes had a vacant look to them. "We haven't slept a wink for three days."

One of the men in the middle Jeep, the Jeep with the four-star license plate, stood up. Suddenly, Gene found himself standing between General George Patton and the exhausted tanker. He tried to be inconspicuous and backed up a few steps. Patton stepped onto the passenger seat and leaned his left hand on the windshield for support. The pearl handles of the revolvers seemed to glow, his helmet glistened in the sunlight, and Gene was taken aback at the intensity of Patton's blue eyes. They were "the bluest of any human" he'd ever seen. Patton was not smiling when he shouted in a distinct, gravel-like voice: "You know there's a war on?"

Patton didn't wait for a reply as he remained standing on the seat, staring at the tank sergeant who returned his stare while fidgeting with his .50-caliber. Apparently losing all semblance of patience, Patton exploded: "I don't give a damn if you haven't slept in a month—I want you down that road!" Patton pointed toward the horizon, "and I don't want to see so much as a single building standing; got that Sergeant?"

Gene backed off a few more steps in the direction of the Opel; he figured he'd lived this long and he wasn't about to get mowed down in a friendly crossfire. He noticed one of the men in the third Jeep cautiously moving for the handles of his .30-caliber, clearly sensing the same danger Gene was experiencing.

Even Billy backed away a few steps, not knowing what the sergeant was likely to do. They both felt he might flip out and start firing at Patton and his entourage. From such a close range he could have easily taken out all three Jeeps before anyone would have had a chance to think, let alone react.

From the look on Patton's face, Gene concluded he had just come to the same realization; Patton slipped back into his seat and said, in a more subdued tone of voice: "I expect you to catch up with me, so get moving!"

Patton's three-Jeep convoy proceeded to turn around and speed their way up the road and out of sight. The sergeant sat there for about a minute then dropped into the turret. Gene and Billy returned to their car and waited until the tank was well ahead of them before continuing on their mission to locate the lost platoon.

Years later, Gene learned, from one of the men in the three Jeeps, Patton had just visited Stalag VII-A and was absolutely infuriated at the manner in which the prisoners had been treated by their German captors. He promised the men: "I'm going to kill every god-damned Nazi from here to Berlin!" His three-Jeep column pulled out of the camp and raced up the road to catch up with the front lines when he stopped to confront the war-weary tank sergeant.

About 15 minutes later, with Patton long out of sight, they encountered a fork in the road and came to an immediate stop. There were no road signs and they lacked a map.

"Which way do you think we should go?" Billy asked.

This photo of Four Star General George Smith Patton, Jr., was believed to be taken while at Stalag VII-A, shortly before he left to catch up with the front line and encountering Gene and a frazzled tanker.

"From the looks of the road everyone's been going left, so let's try going right. Maybe that's where your lost platoon went."

They took the road less traveled, which cut through a dense, beautiful forest. In a matter of minutes they came around a bend and found themselves facing a double column of about 130 German soldiers. Gene stopped the car a mere 30 feet from the head of the column and looked them over. To his chagrin he realized they appeared to be just about the toughest, meanest-looking, battle-hardened veterans he'd ever come across. He was relieved when he realized they were not "SS"; however, with only one rifle between them, fighting was not going to be feasible, and Gene considered the possibility his luck had finally run out.

"Should we fight?" Billy asked.

"What, with one rifle and a bunch of swords? Stay calm and follow me."

Gene exited the car along with Billy who was holding his rifle to his side instead of slung over his shoulder. They stood in front of the car as the commanding officer, a colonel with a mildly scarred, weary-looking face, surprised them both when he raised his arms and shouted: *"Kamarads!"*

Gene asked him if he spoke *"Englander,"* to which he responded: "Yes I do."

Gene noticed there was something odd about the men lined up behind the colonel. After a couple moments he realized they weren't armed.

"Where's all your weapons?" Gene asked.

The colonel motioned to a nearby hillside and explained they had been dug in, waiting for the Americans. When he decided it was time to surrender the men left their guns behind. He continued to explain they had been by-passed by the Americans and he felt there could only be a few days remaining before Germany's formal surrender. With the war clearly lost, he had no desire to lose any more of his troops. He said: "Why continue?"

Gene told him: "You guys will be home before we will," to which the colonel shook his head in relieved agreement.

Gene asked him how long they had been encamped there. The colonel explained they'd been dug in for three days. From time to time they heard tanks but none ever appeared. He mentioned something about the Führer's death, then said: "I would like to surrender my forces to you at this time." The colonel removed his Luger side-arm and offered it to Gene, who declined to accept the gun. Billy was quick to reach over and take it for himself, at which point Gene replied to the colonel's offer of surrender: "Well Colonel, that sounds pretty swell, except we're in kind of a hurry. You haven't happened to see a platoon of black American soldiers around here, have you?"

Slightly surprised, the colonel, standing not more than 2 feet from Gene, replied: "No, you are the first I've encountered." He paused as he looked Gene directly in the eye and said: "*Kamarad,* kindly accept my surrender."

"I'm really sorry Colonel, but I have an agenda to keep so here's what you do. Have your men get all their weapons and stack them on the side of the road. Then march your men with their hands behind their heads straight up this road. When you get to Moosburg the very first thing you're going to see is a firehouse. You and your men take up camp there and hang out a bunch of white flags so nobody gets the wrong idea and someone will come along and pick all of you up."

The colonel appeared puzzled. Following a few moments' thought he shrugged his shoulders and turned to one of his officers. He gave him orders directing the men to retrieve their weapons and stack them alongside the road, unaware the reason Gene wanted them to stack their guns was to assure himself they were not booby-trapped. It was at that point Billy noticed the colonel's backpack was made of deerskin and said to him he'd really like the backpack. Gene grabbed Billy's arm and whispered in his ear: "Listen, we should just get the hell out of here while we can. No need to press things."

Almost before Gene stopped talking, the colonel began to slip off his backpack. He called over several soldiers to hold the contents as he carefully emptied his pack. When he was finished, he smiled and handed the backpack to Billy, explaining it would "be confiscated anyway." Billy was absolutely thrilled to have it.

As they turned to walk back to the car, Billy quietly asked Gene if he had noticed the soldiers' eyes.

"I sure did. They looked hollow, almost as if someone's stolen their very souls." Billy paused for a moment and asked: "Why'd you make them stack their rifles?"

"Just wanted to be sure they weren't booby-trapped."

They quickly walked to the car, got in, turned it around, and immediately drove back to the fork in the road lest the colonel change his mind. As they drove away, Gene smiled when he looked into the rearview mirror and noticed a couple of the soldiers emptying their backpacks onto the ground and transferring the colonel's belongings into them. Apparently the colonel decided giving up his backpack was one thing, but he wasn't going to leave his possessions behind.

When they returned to the fork in the road they turned left, knowing the missing platoon could not possibly have taken the fork to the right. A few miles further up the road they came upon a farmhouse where Gene concluded the lost platoon was likely bivouacked. There were two stacks of M1 rifles, five or six to a stack, along with additional M1's leaning against a water trough located near the open front door to the farmhouse.

Encountering no sentries, Gene and Billy went inside in search of the platoon's lieutenant. Gene pointed to a man sitting at the kitchen table, while an older woman was hard at work standing over a cast iron stove frying chicken in a large iron skillet alongside boiling pots of vegetables. The mood in the room was light as the men were taking a deserved rest.

"Billy, he must be the man you're looking for."

"Yeah, but what are you goin' to do now, Gene?"

"I've got a little lady waiting for me in München; maybe we'll catch up with each other back in DeKalb."

"Good luck Gene. It was really swell to see you again and thanks for the ride. Oh, I guess this time I should say, 'I'll see you back in DeKalb.'"

The two men smiled at the memory of Billy poking his head out of the science classroom and shook hands. As Gene strode back to the Opel he glanced behind him and saw Billy walking over to the lieutenant. Gene returned to the car determined to get himself to München, then on to Paris, in his words: "lickety-split."

CHAPTER TWENTY-TWO

Paris via München

Gene struck out for Paris, leaving Billy behind to carry on with his mission. He intended to make a stop in München first and visit the beautiful young lady he met on the train. He encountered only occasional traffic and was in between towns when he noticed a civilian standing a short distance up the roadside. It struck him as unusual, because he was holding his hands over his head. Gene instinctively slowed down, though he had no intention of stopping. He knew a certain degree of lawlessness existed in the vacuum between the as-yet unconquered Germany and a newly occupied Germany. Aware former Russian POWs could show up anywhere, he was not going to take any unnecessary chances.

As he drew closer the man lowered his hands and a second man wearing a raggedy Russian uniform suddenly appeared from behind him and stood at attention, saluting toward Gene. He slowed a little further but didn't stop. After he passed them he looked into the rearview mirror and noticed the civilian's hands were back in the air and the Russian, probably a former prisoner of war, was robbing him. He had yet to come face-to-face with a Russian, though they continued to appear individually and in small groups, just often enough to keep Gene on the alert.

He thought it was strange how Russians would pop up out of nowhere so deep behind the American front lines and wondered why they weren't on their way home to their Motherland. Later, in a conversation with a former Russian prisoner of war he would encounter in Paris, Gene would learn they had nowhere to go: if they returned to Russia they'd either be worked to death in a gulag or shot outright. The Russian explained to him they were considered traitors to the Motherland for having allowed themselves to be captured.

Gene was excited at the prospect of traveling into München on his own free will rather than packed inside of a freight car. The weather was good as he entered the outskirts of the city and the prospect of spending some leisure time with the young woman he met on the train put him into a particularly good frame of mind. Once he was in München proper, he was perplexed as both sides of the roads were lined with parked cars. In all his trips into the city as a prisoner of war it was rare to see one civilian car, let alone scores of them lining the roads.

As he approached the first major intersection he encountered a number of "spiffy-looking" white-helmeted Military Police directing traffic. One of them was blowing his whistle and directing Gene to make a right-hand turn. At the very next intersection yet another MP was indicating for him to turn again. Gene slowed the car as he realized there were parked cars everywhere and the MPs likely intended to confiscate his borrowed Opel. He thought to himself: "Damn, there goes München!" He had only a moment to consider the fact he was not going to make it to the beautiful young woman's home as he was quickly approaching a road block.

A diagonal set of railroad tracks leading out of town lay between him and the next MP, who was vigorously waving at him. Ignoring the MP, he turned left onto the tracks and began to drive away at the best speed he could make, the MP "blowing his brains out" with his whistle and waving his arms over his head as hard as he could. Gene smiled as he said aloud: "Hello, Paris!"

Once he was safely out of sight, he slipped into an empty garage and decided to wait until dark. He was no longer afraid of Allied bombers or German patrols; instead, he needed to dodge the MPs. At first light he pulled back onto the highway; from then on, he would travel only on side roads, which quickly proved to be free of Military Police.

Lacking a road map, he couldn't determine the best alternate course to Paris so he parked and waited. After a short delay he flagged down a Jeep and asked the lieutenant sitting in the front passenger seat if he could spare a map. Recognizing him as a former POW he happily gave him a good road map, another 10–1 ration box, some chocolate bars, and a carton of cigarettes. A sergeant sitting in the back of the Jeep mentioned Gene might "make use of the soap" in the rations, just in case he wasn't aware he stood out like a sore thumb in his dirty, blood-stained, dilapidated uniform. Gene smiled, thanked him for the advice, and returned to his borrowed Opel.

He spent a few minutes studying the map and eventually found himself facing a pontoon bridge over the Rhine River at Mannheim, Germany—the same pontoon bridge General Patton had ventured upon only days earlier. France lay on the other side of the bridge, which appeared to be his last major obstacle before Paris. As he approached the bridge, an MP standing sentry duty waved for him to stop, walked up to his car, and said:

"Just where the hell do ya think you're going Joe?" He wore a pistol and had left his rifle leaning against the guard shack. Gene noticed his uniform was "quite spiffy" and the sentry's face told him the man had not seen any combat as he appeared far too innocent.

"I'm going to Paris," Gene replied in a matter-of-fact manner.

"You can't cross the Rhine; there's a war on, you know!"

Gene reached behind him, grabbed one of the firemen's swords from under the orange canvas cover, and said: "I hate to do this but I really need to get across the Rhine." Gene pulled one sword from the back seat and let the MP have a good look at it. "I took this from a Nazi officer; just let me cross and it's yours."

The sentry's eyes opened wide as he accepted the sword and without further protest stepped back from the car and said: "This'll only get you to the other side Joe. There's an MP over there and he'll probably send you back."

"Either way, the sword's yours." As Gene put the car in gear he added: "I'll take my chances."

He took off across the bridge and, after bribing the sentry on the French side of the Rhine with yet another sword, continued on his way to Paris. It was getting late and he was tired and hungry. He spotted a farmhouse with lights on inside and smoke coming from a chimney so he pulled up to the front door. The farmer, his wife, and children were all quite happy to see him, in part because he was American and in part because he was carrying a box of 10–1 rations. They wined him, dined him, and gave up one of their beds for him to sleep in. He considered it to be a very pleasant welcome to France and a good omen.

In the morning the farmer urged him to spend a few days as their guest of honor. Gene declined as politely as he could and indicated he needed to see his friend in Paris, Doctor LaBorde. They insisted he stay for breakfast, and since he couldn't eat too much at a time, the farmer's wife gave him a small basket of freshly baked biscuits to take with him. He thanked her profusely as he had always been fond of biscuits and hers were the best he'd eaten.

As he drove along the countryside he passed what appeared to be a mile-long stack of artillery shells. They were a few feet deep and a few feet high, creating what turned out to be a convenient, though potentially explosive, wall between the road and the farm's fields.

About mid-morning he arrived in Paris and immediately sought out the chateau of Doctor LaBorde. He parked his Opel about a block from his residence and was walking over to his house when a pair of Military Police abruptly stopped him. Gene explained he was on his way to see his friend, Dr. LaBorde. Refusing to believe him, the two MPs accused Gene of being a deserter and unceremoniously hauled him to their headquarters. They brought him before their commanding officer who, most likely, was Lieutenant Colonel James B. Ramage. Ramage looked at Gene and immediately noticed he was wearing prisoner-of-war tags around his neck. He turned his attention to the two MPs and said: "What the hell are you two knuckleheads doing?" He was not talking gently but lowered his voice significantly when he turned to address Gene.

"Son, take a seat, relax, and tell me what the hell are you doing in Paris?"

Gene told Ramage he'd just arrived, following the liberation of Stalag VII-A. He described his overnight jail stay in München, having come on the heels of his unsuccessful escape attempt. He said that's where he met Doctor LaBorde. Gene explained LaBorde lived just a couple of blocks away and he had an open invitation to spend some time with him and enjoy Paris.

The colonel listened intently then ordered the MPs to get Gene a shower, a haircut, a shave, and a new uniform. He also ordered them to make sure they arranged for him to have some hot chow. Though Gene did have breakfast at the farm and had consumed the biscuits he took with him over the course of the morning, he was, in fact, quite hungry.

Ramage also arranged for Gene to immediately receive a partial draw on his backpay. In a few hours Gene looked as if he were a new man, and with some money in his pockets, he was in very high spirits, eager to explore all Paris had to offer. Each breath he took felt better than the one before. Gene proceeded directly to LaBorde's chateau where he was greeted as if the two men were long-lost family.

LaBorde didn't waste any time taking Gene to all his favorite cafés, bars, and places of interest but immediately recognized the Opel, at that point lacking the orange tarp, was a likely target for the MPs. He cleverly crafted an official-looking "82nd Airborne Staff News" placard, added a pair of undecipherable signatures, and placed it in the windshield. Nobody questioned them thereafter and the two men freely drove about Paris.

LaBorde proved to have a voracious appetite for women, wine, cheese, and especially, food and music. He also required very little sleep which suited Gene "just fine," as the excitement of freedom proved to be a huge motivator. He discovered reserves of energy he thought were long gone and experienced no difficulty keeping pace with LaBorde.

Gene quickly found himself engulfed in a whirlwind of semi-extravagant indulgences. On May 8, 1945, the day the Allied High Command announced Germany had surrendered, the two men joined the crowds dancing in the streets of Paris as the entire city celebrated Victory in Europe.

One evening LaBorde mentioned he had heard of a bizarre performance taking place in one of the private clubs and thought they should go and see it for themselves. Gene shrugged his shoulders as if to say, "why not?" The two friends immediately embarked on a 30-minute walk down side streets until they found themselves turning into an alley in an off-the-beaten-path part of the city.

Halfway through the alley they came upon the entrance to the club. Except for a small printed sign on the gray door, it looked just like any other door on the block. Guarding the entrance was a rather large, unshaven man wearing a black hat pulled halfway down his face. His black hair flipped up from the sides of the cap, making him, in Gene's opinion, appear a bit comical. He was sporting a double-breasted black overcoat, with his right hand ominously shoved into a pocket, suggesting he might be armed. Once LaBorde paid him the requisite fee, he stepped aside, opened the door, and let them through without ever saying a word.

Gene and LaBorde followed a long hallway and eventually walked into a semi-darkened room full of round tables occupied by well-dressed men and women, four persons to a table. There were also a number of American and French military officers present. They sat at an empty table, perhaps 3 feet away from the curtainless stage, ordered a bottle of wine, and settled in. After some time passed a man in a tuxedo strolled onto the stage and announced the first act, which happened to be the act LaBorde was curious to witness.

In a few moments a man in a black trench coat slowly walked to the center of the stage. He said nothing and his face was without emotion. Gene and LaBorde looked at each other as if to say: "What's with this guy?"

A couple of the audience members shouted out a few derogatory remarks, which drew a dead-panned response from him to the effect: "Please, I need absolute quiet or I cannot concentrate." The audience grew silent. LaBorde appeared fascinated, while Gene was ready to walk out as he found the guests more interesting to look at than the actor on stage. Their second bottle of wine had just arrived and his host had paid for their admission so he poured himself another glass and decided he'd "wait it out."

The man's act proved to be singularly boring and a waste of their precious time. Once they finished the second bottle LaBorde promised to make it up to him and took them to a lively cabaret for the balance of the evening. The event was so completely weird and off-the-wall Gene never forgot it.

In the roughly 10 or so days Gene spent in Paris he drove past the Louvre literally every day. Not only did he make no attempt to enter it, he never even noticed if it was open. LaBorde kept them on the run from dawn until deep into the night, as he made certain his American friend would be thoroughly exposed to everything Paris had to offer, including the women.

He exhausted his supply of swords as trading material but had managed to retain the ornate silver stein the farmer's wife in Moosburg had given to him as he intended to bring it home. Thanks to LaBorde's generosity he still had a little cash when he announced it was probably time for him to seek passage back to the United States. LaBorde, after failing to convince him to stay a little longer, bid him a tearful farewell and insisted they stop for one last drink together.

Before he could leave Paris Gene had two final things to accomplish. First, he went to the Western Union office and telegraphed his parents he would be "home sometime this summer." Second, he desired to make a final stop at what had become his favorite bar.

While sitting at the bar having a "goodbye to Paris glass of wine" with LaBorde, an Army Air Force captain took a seat next to Gene and offered to buy them another round. The three men engaged in conversation, the captain finding himself captivated with Gene's story and LaBorde's depth of knowledge regarding the best places to experience in Paris. The conversation eventually steered toward what Gene planned to do with the Opel. Gene told him he had no title and no keys, and, without really giving the matter any thought, blurted out: "I'd take 600 dollars for it." Much to his surprise and delight the captain replied: "I can get you the cash but I need to go back to Orly for it." Gene replied: "We can wait."

The captain laid some money on the bar and told them to have another drink. He said he would return in a little while. About an hour later he reappeared and ordered the bartender to bring a fresh round. They proceeded to complete the transaction and finish the wine.

About 20 minutes later the three men exited the bar. The captain got into the Opel and began to drive away while Gene and LaBorde started walking in the opposite direction. It wasn't long before Gene heard the familiar sound of MPs blowing their whistles. They turned, looked behind them, and noticed a number of white-helmeted MPs had surrounded the captain and were examining the Opel. Gene urged LaBorde to pick up the pace as he wanted nothing to do with whatever was going on. As they disappeared around the corner Gene heard the captain calling out to them: "Hey, fellas! Come back!"

While Gene never intended to do anything other than abandon the car, he sure did need the money. He rationalized he had held up his end of the bargain and made no representations of ownership, leaving him with a clear conscience—and 600 dollars.

Later the same day a couple of MPs noticed his uniform was a bit unusual, for it lacked any identifying patches. He was wearing a simple shirt and pants, though his practically worn-out boots were still the same ones he had been issued back in the United States and were a stark contrast to his fresh uniform. They demanded he produce a pass, which was impossible, and they accused him of being AWOL. Gene thought to himself he might still be listed as AWOL from the hospital back in England. He offered up his POW dog tags as evidence he was a POW, but in Gene's words, "they didn't buy it" and ordered him to: "Come with us."

They wasted no time escorting him and an additional POW they picked up along the way before another colonel who was nowhere near as understanding as Colonel Ramage had been. He looked at Gene and his new companion as if they were some manner of criminals and burst out: "We're going to get all you sons-of-bitches back into custody where you belong!"

Gene responded: "But we aren't AWOL." He pulled out his Stalag VII-A dog tags and held them up for the colonel to inspect—except the colonel didn't seem to care and further admonished them: "You two are going to be on the next boat back to the U.S. I want both of you here promptly at 0800 hours tomorrow. Understood?"

The two men responded in unison: "Yes, Sir!"

Gene and his new friend quickly left the building and speculated the MPs were having a hard time believing they were former POWs since both of them had been showered and shaved. Gene again recalled the poster at Camp Grant prodding the men to "Look your best." He considered it was one time looking his best didn't work out.

Following a raucous night in Paris Gene and his pal slept late into the following morning, and by the time they managed to show up at the colonel's office it was closer to 1300 hours than 0800 hours. The colonel decided to take no further chances on losing track of them and ordered an MP to stay with the men until they boarded a truck to Camp "Lucky Strike," located a little to the northeast of the French port of Le Havre.

Camp "Lucky Strike" was one of a series of so-called "cigarette camps," each camp being named after a popular brand of cigarettes. They were large tent cities designed to serve as temporary housing for servicemen returning home until their respective ships were ready to depart for the east coast of the United States. It wasn't long after Gene arrived at "Lucky Strike" that he found himself on a dock in Le Havre.

CHAPTER TWENTY-THREE

Home at Last

Le Havre proved to be an old-style port city and nothing like Paris. Crowded with soldiers, sailors, former POWs, deserters from all sides, and locals, it lacked the class of Paris but didn't lack for bars.

Gene heard the Germans had constructed massive concrete bunkers from which they operated their U-boat war against Allied shipping. He wasn't necessarily interested in seeing them. Instead, he felt the need to enjoy himself a little longer and took a stroll around the harbor area, stopping off now and again for a glass of wine before it was time to board a Liberty ship for the snail-paced, approximately 18-day voyage to the United States.

Later the same afternoon he sought out the Liberty ship to which he was assigned and learned it wouldn't be boarding until the following morning. He decided that, rather than return to "Lucky Strike" for the night, he'd simply sleep on the dock where hundreds of other servicemen were doing the same thing.

When he woke up the next day he discovered someone had stolen the beautiful silver beer stein, given to him by the housewife in Moosburg, from his gunny sack. He looked around for the culprit but whoever had stolen it was probably long gone and soon it was time to board the ship; he shrugged it off as yet another lesson learned the hard way.

The Liberty ship was both much smaller and a great deal slower than the *Queen Elizabeth*. It was also every bit as crowded, but it had an American crew with American grub served three times a day.

Music was piped through the ship's speakers around the clock, creating a need for disc jockeys to select and play the hundreds of options available. Gene figured it would be a lot more interesting than standing around all day and shooting the breeze so he volunteered to take the job. The most popular song among the former prisoners of war was the Cole Porter song "Don't Fence Me In" performed by Bing Crosby and the Andrews Sisters. He sometimes played the song nonstop for hours, though he and his volunteer assistant, Charlie, had stacks of "78 rpm" records from which to choose.

There was a fairly solid stream of fellow passengers stopping in to make special requests, resulting in Gene and Charlie spending a lot of time alphabetizing the record collection to make facilitating the scores of requests less tedious. Despite the flood of requests, Gene still managed to dominate the "air waves" with "Don't Fence Me In."

Early on the first Sunday morning at sea, during what would prove to be a nearly three-week voyage, one of the ship's padres came into the studio carrying an album of religious songs. He handed it to Gene and stated: "I want you to play this at 1100 hours, sharp!"

"Sure, Padre," Gene replied.

A couple of minutes before 1100 hours, Gene looked at Charlie, held up the album of church music, and said: "Do we really want to play this?"

"Hell no!" exclaimed Charlie, who opened the porthole and indicated Gene should throw the album overboard, which he did. About 15 minutes later the padre, appearing somewhat troubled, returned.

"Where's my music?" His tone was more demanding than questioning.

Gene glanced at the clock as if he'd lost track of time and replied: "Oh yeah! Hold on Padre, it'll be right on." Gene looked at Charlie as if he were responsible and said: "Charlie, where'd you put the padre's album?"

"I haven't seen it since he brought it in," Charlie replied, forcing himself to appear genuinely concerned.

The two men began searching through the stacks of albums pretending to be searching for the padre's selection. After a couple minutes of impatiently watching them flipping through scores of albums, with no success, the padre noticed the porthole was open. Realizing what they must have done he threw his hands up into the air in disgust and left, never to return.

Gene felt the trip was agonizingly long, as the Liberty ships were not designed for speed or comfort. Eighteen very long days after departing

France the ship docked in Newport News, Rhode Island. Gene, though only a short train excursion from New York, a city he had yet to experience, bee-lined for the nearest railroad station to commence a series of train rides taking him to his assigned destination, the Army base at Fort Sheridan, Illinois. He spent a few days at Fort Sheridan for "processing" and received a new uniform, along with orders to report to Miami Beach, Florida, in September. His uniform was the only clothing he possessed; consequently, he wore it continuously and enjoyed the side benefit of people treating him to drinks and food throughout the entire trip.

When he finally arrived home in DeKalb it was in the same manner he left it back in 1942: hitch-hiking. His parents had no idea he was coming and when he walked into his clapboard house and found his mother working in the kitchen, he said: "Hi Mom, what's up?"

It was late May or perhaps the first of June, 1945.

In September Gene decided he'd better finish high school. In those days there were no short-cuts to a high school diploma; consequently, he found himself back at DeKalb High. Much to his chagrin, he also had to finish his math class, which meant dealing with Mr. Hoppe.

One night in late September 1945 Gene wandered into the DeKalb Elks Club, grabbed a beer, and noticed a few of the guys were playing cards. Not being much of a card player, he pulled up a chair and decided he'd watch the game for a bit. It was dark in the room, so initially he didn't get a clear look at everyone sitting around the card table.

After he watched them finish the round and as the dealer was shuffling the deck, Gene noticed Mr. Hoppe was one of the players. Several rounds were subsequently played. Men were getting up and down to replenish their drinks. There had been precious little extraneous conversation and Gene and Hoppe had yet to acknowledge each other.

Eventually it was Hoppe's turn to decide whether he needed to draw a card. He picked up his cards, held them just below his eyes, and stared directly at Gene.

"Gene, did you do your homework?" Hoppe asked, matter-of-factly.

Gene couldn't hide his smile as he replied: "Yes, Sir, I most certainly did!"

CHAPTER TWENTY-FOUR

Postwar Life

Gene's folks let him know he was welcome to stay as long as he wanted without paying them rent so there was no pressure on him to immediately seek employment. In fact, he had yet to formulate anything resembling career goals, so he worked at odd jobs throughout the summer for pocket change. He spent his spare time hanging out with returning veterans at a local pub by the name of "McCabe's."

Never one to miss the opportunity to throw a party, Gene and one of his newly made veteran friends decided to hold a reunion and began inviting all the returning veterans in the vicinity. The event took on ever greater proportions when both the local American Legion and Veterans of Foreign Wars groups decided to contribute their support to the effort. Even the City of DeKalb became involved, when it voluntarily opened up Hopkins Park as the event site, free of charge. The reunion was a big success, resulting in Gene and his friend donating the 600 dollars in net proceeds they collected from ticket sales equally between the Legion and the VFW.

He was still in active service and his next assignment required he report to Miami Beach, Florida, for two weeks of rest and relaxation in a luxury beachfront hotel on the first of September. His stay was somewhat interrupted by the "Homestead" hurricane. As he recalls: "I never saw coconuts move so fast."

After Miami Beach he was sent to the Army Air Force regional hospital in Coral Gables, Florida. He mulled over the fact he was booted from Stalag Luft III because he was considered infantry, yet he was sent to

Gene with his father, June 1945.

an Army Air Corps hospital. He thought: "Go figure!" The doctors examined his ears, but at the time they didn't have a procedure to address his shattered right eardrum. They told him he'd just have to live with it. Oddly, nobody mentioned his high blood pressure.

Years later a doctor at a Veterans Administration hospital in California attempted to rebuild the eardrum, but the procedure failed. Since the night he was left for dead at Nijmegen, Holland, Gene has been without hearing in his right ear and requires a hearing aid in his left ear, both hearing deficiencies courtesy of a German "88."

While at Coral Gables he inquired as to his Purple Heart and was met with: "You need to get us the names of the medics who attended to you." The reality, of course, was he had received a cursory exam by a German medic, which made conforming to the request impossible. Needless to say, he never received his Purple Heart.

At the time of his discharge the 508th was still in Germany, while he was home for good. Gene heard his old division had been, in his words, "all spruced up," and was serving as the honor guard for General

Note the absence of a "Purple Heart" and Bronze Star among Gene's awards. There was no medal or ribbon for putting his life in extreme peril to save the life of critically injured fellow paratrooper Elmer Melchi at Stalag XII-A or for his head and hearing injury incurred at Nijmegen. He is, however, very proud of his good conduct ribbon.

Dwight Eisenhower. Consequently, he knew they probably didn't have it too bad over there but strongly preferred being home.

Gene was discharged from the Army by the United States Army Air Force while he was at Coral Gables. He figured Colonel Spivey had not been consulted or they may have sent him back to Fort Sheridan for the discharge, because, after all, he was infantry. This time, instead of a train ride to hell, he returned to DeKalb in a comfortable Pullman car.

Upon his return he enrolled at DeKalb High School as a senior. In January or February 1946 the principal called him into his office one morning and advised him there was a "new test" available and if he passed he would receive the equivalent of a high school degree. He handed Gene a slip with the time and place he was to take the exam and told him: "Be there!"

Gene, rather uncharacteristically, showed up on time, sat for the test and resumed attending high school classes. One morning, a few weeks later, he was again called into the principal's office. The principal looked him over once and said: "Well, you're through with high school." He paused as if considering whether he should say anything further, and continued: "You know, you're a lot older than the other students..." His voice trailed off for a moment when he abruptly blurted out: "Turn in your books and goodbye!"

Immediately after his final moments as a high school senior he was on his way to McCabe's Tavern. As he casually strolled down the street, his mind drifted to a phrase his father often said: "Hollywood is nothing but a house of ill-repute, without a roof!"

It was enough motivation to spur Gene to travel to California to see for himself. When he arrived in the Los Angeles train depot he had five dollars to his name. He had broken up with Betty and had no friends in California. For him the number one factor was pretty simple: "Nobody was shooting at me." He said: "Lights were on and people were being people."

He immediately landed a job at a large aircraft company in Burbank and proceeded to settle in. There was one thing he knew with certainty: he wasn't going to spend his life spraying zinc chromate on airplanes. Gene had become aware he could go to college on something called the "GI Bill," so he looked into how he could take advantage of the program.

In his spare time he had been playing baseball on a local team dominated by members of the UCLA college squad. They urged him to attend UCLA and play ball there. He thought about it and decided he'd like to attend UCLA and play baseball. As it happened, the UCLA baseball coach had already seen him play and wanted him on the team. At his request Gene sent for his high school transcripts as he'd need them for the enrollment process.

As it turned out, Gene had what UCLA baseball coach Art Reichle deemed "certain high school deficiencies." Gene would need to attend junior college and address the "deficiencies" one at a time. The deficiencies constituted classes he skipped as a result of obtaining his high school equivalency certificate. Reichle suggested Gene enroll in El Camino Junior College and take the required classes there while simultaneously playing for the junior college's baseball team.

Gene soon discovered the El Camino baseball team was loaded with players destined to play for USC. The El Camino baseball coaches were all former USC athletes. When Rod "Bud" Dedeaux, the USC head

Gene (top row, second from right, wearing glasses) as a member of the USC baseball team.

baseball coach, saw him play, Gene found himself being recruited to attend USC. Gene jumped at the opportunity. However, acceptance was not automatic. After graduating El Camino Junior College, Coach Dedeaux sent him to Susanville, California, to play on an amateur baseball team located there for the summer. In the interim his application for enrollment worked its way through the system, and he was eventually accepted into USC for the fall semester.

As much as he enjoyed playing baseball for USC, and especially for coach Dedeaux, he eventually had to make a decision. Between practices and games, half of the games being on the road, his grades were beginning to suffer. He didn't know what to do until he considered something he had overheard his dad say, when a friend asked him what Gene intended to be when he got out of college. His father had replied: "An old man."

Bearing in mind his father's potentially prophetic words, Gene took stock of himself. He was decidedly older than his teammates, which made it difficult for him to bond with them. He thought it might be nice to go into teaching, as it would offer him better long-term security than did baseball. He decided to quit USC's baseball team and eventually earned his degree in Fine Arts.

He took a teaching position at Mountain View High School in Mountain View, California, and coached the baseball, basketball, and football teams in addition to his teaching chores. While there he became fast friends with Sid Hall, who would eventually be wooed by John Madden to join the Oakland Raiders' coaching staff.

One night he and some friends found themselves in a San Francisco area night club. They were dancing with their respective dates when someone firmly elbowed him in his lower back. He didn't think much of it, though it happened a second time. He continued to ignore the wayward dancer until it happened a third time. He stopped, turned around, and looked down. The offending elbow belonged to the height-challenged actor Edward G. Robinson who looked up at him, smiled, shrugged his shoulders, and said: "Sorry." Gene smiled back at him and continued dancing.

Gene eventually married. He and his wife Paulette took advantage of the fact Gene, as a teacher, had summers off. They decided to make a trip to Europe and revisit some of his World War II haunts. While taking a tour of a Hewlett-Packard facility in Burlington, Austria, sometime in 1961, Gene ran into another paratrooper veteran of Nijmegen, "Captain Jack." Jack wasn't on the American side during the war and actually was one of the German Fallschirmjägers defending Nijmegen. He was eventually captured about 2 miles west of the road bridge.

Gene explained he had observed a Fallschirmjäger captain after he had been captured. Jack stated it couldn't have been him, as he was a few kilometers away at the time. Gene and his wife joined Captain Jack and his wife the same evening at Captain Jack's residence and reviewed Jack's World War II photos. It struck Gene how similar the photos were to his own experiences on the American side, the only difference being the uniforms.

During the evening Captain Jack described how, at the onset of Operation *Market Garden*, one of his men came across a satchel which contained the complete plans for the operation in an abandoned glider. He immediately realized what they represented and personally presented the satchel to Field Marshal Walter Model. Model, as in the movie *A Bridge Too Far*, thought the plans were fake. Captain Jack took it upon himself to make certain every detail set forth in the captured plans was conveyed to as many units in the field as he could and made it clear to Gene: "It was no accident we over-ran planned drop-zones and were waiting for your paratroopers as they arrived over the course of the following days."

He further explained when the Polish Brigade dropped into their landing zone they were met with "devastating fire" from a prepared defense. Captain Jack wouldn't speculate what might have happened in the event Model had realized the plans were genuine and immediately acted on them himself.

A side-bar to the story is the French held Captain Jack as a POW for five years after the end of the war, until one day they simply told him to "go home." He walked the entire distance. Upon arriving home he re-enlisted in the army and was appointed as the military commandant of Burlington. He served for three years before joining Hewlett-Packard to commence his civilian life.

Gene and Paulette traveled to Nijmegen, as Gene felt a strong need to revisit the castle where he had been interrogated. Much to their mutual delight the castle was still there, in great condition, and was home to a white tablecloth restaurant, "The Belvedere," located on the top floor of the tower. Of course they made dinner reservations.

The dining room in the tower was not very large, with seating around the outer walls and a handful of tables scattered across the middle of the

A World War II German Fallschirmjäger badge.

room. Gene and his wife chose a table in the center of the room, allowing them a view of the entire dining room. They could even see the River Waal through the windows. There were no empty tables and a number of diners had looked at them with a bit of curiosity. They all continued with their meals while engaging in quiet conversation as Gene and his wife settled into their seats. Before their drinks arrived Gene called his waiter over and asked him quite bluntly: "Didn't Heinrich Himmler use this place as his headquarters during the war?"

The waiter appeared to be dumbstruck as the entire dining area immediately fell dead silent. Without responding, the waiter scooted off to confer with the *maître d'*. A couple of minutes later the waiter returned and asked: "Sir, why do you ask about Herr Himmler?"

During the interim nobody in the room was speaking as everyone was staring at the American couple as if they were from another planet.

Gene responded, loud enough for all to hear: "Well, I was in a parachute regiment and was dropped into Nijmegen as part of *Market Garden* back in '44. I was captured not far from here on the first night and they brought me here to be interrogated by Himmler. He was in a large, rectangular room with plush, deep red carpeting at the end of a spiral staircase leading to the basement."

"Were you a general?" asked the waiter.

Gene laughed and shook his head.

The waiter relaxed and responded: "Yes, Herr Himmler did use this castle. He made frequent trips here during the war and, yes, the castle was his headquarters. The rectangular room where you were interrogated is still there. We use it for storage now. We don't talk much about him or the war really."

Appearing relieved, the waiter left and returned shortly with their drink order.

They enjoyed a great steak dinner as Gene marveled how much difference the years had made. Throughout the evening his fellow diners would step up and thank him for fighting on their behalf against the Germans. Gene's money proved to be no good in Nijmegen, as the restaurant refused to accept any manner of payment from him. There was no leaving him for dead by the friendly people of Nijmegen.

When they checked into their Nijmegen hotel Gene poked his head into the bar. A balding, somewhat rotund man was polishing the bar-top and merrily singing a song. Gene sat at the bar and, over a couple of beers, on the house, learned the bartender was the owner of the hotel and had been the top man in the World War II Dutch underground organization that went by the moniker "Nameless." He arranged for the Bürgermeister of Groesbeek, Holland, to take Gene to the drop zone.

Gene met the Bürgermeister and found him more than happy to drive him to the drop zone. He explained to Gene he'd been living in Groesbeek at the time of *Market Garden* and was extremely familiar with the history of the operation. With little direction from Gene, he drove him to within 20 feet of the spot where he had touched down. The house which played host to a game of cat and mouse between a German infantryman and a parachuting sergeant was still there and was occupied. There was no longer any sign of the antiaircraft installations. Standing in the field, years later, afforded him the opportunity to put the experience into perspective.

The following morning they crossed the bridge over the River Waal to Lent. He located the house where he, a German corporal, and an American sergeant had spent a night huddled in a fireplace during an artillery barrage. Though the house was once again being used as a residence, the tree which had blocked his exit was still there. Of the fallen branches, just enough of them had been cut away to allow entrance through the front door.

Years later he would meet up with his buddy Ray Meade at a reunion. Meade was astonished, and thrilled, to see him alive. Meade described to him what actually transpired at Nijmegen when Gene had been knocked unconscious. He explained he was absolutely certain Gene was dead. Up until then Gene had always assumed they had either abandoned him or all of them had been killed. They picked up their friendship as if there had been no intervening decades and it continues to this day.

Billy Carey apparently never went back to DeKalb and Gene never saw him again. He tried looking him up a few times, but to no avail.

In the 1960s, while on a golf outing in Fountain Hills, Arizona, Gene met Jessie, one of General Patton's escorts from the day he encountered

This picture was a gift from Jessie, the man wearing a helmet, third from the right behind General Patton, in the center of the photo. According to Jessie, General Patton had "saved all his piss" for the Rhine. Patton had just about finished relieving himself when a reporter took the photo. Jessie confiscated the film and directed the general's photo team to make just one copy. Apparently the team made a few copies for themselves. Jessie allowed Gene to make, and retain, a copy of his original photograph.

Gene and the stressed-out Sherman tanker. Remarkably, Jessie did recall the encounter and mentioned he remembered there were a couple of GIs standing nearby. He particularly remembered that one of the GIs, in his words, "looked like a mess." He confirmed he felt the tank sergeant was unstable and was relieved when Patton toned it down in response to his pleading whispers: "General, General." He relayed to Gene how infuriated Patton was at the condition of the prisoners of war and had exclaimed: "I'm going to kill every god-damned Nazi from here to Berlin!" He said to characterize Patton as being in a foul mood when he came upon the resting tanker "would be understatement."

Gene stayed in touch with Jessie until his passing.

At a luncheon reunion of POWs in Mesa, Arizona, sometime in the 1970s, Gene ran into the barber from his barracks. He was the same man who had been charging one cigarette for a haircut when liberation was pending. They were going over old times when Gene mentioned the pregnant black cat and wondered what became of it. The barber and two other former POWs looked at each other and, following a brief pause, the barber laughed as he exclaimed: "We ate it!"

Gene replied: "I guess it wasn't as free as I thought. I'm darned glad I didn't know about it back then."

On another occasion, Gene was teaching an evening art class at a college in Colorado Springs, Colorado, when a particularly strong snowstorm began to develop. He looked out the windows and declared class was ending early so the students wouldn't get snowed in.

As he drove home he decided to stop in a lounge near the south gate of the Air Force Academy, where he came upon two Air Force Academy cadets at the bar conversing with a civilian. Gene overheard the civilian tell them he'd been shot down while flying a bombing raid over the Ploesti Oil Fields in Romania and had been transported to Stalag VII-A. The cadets soon departed, leaving the civilian, Gene, and the bartender the only persons remaining and, in Gene's words, "stupid enough" to ignore the snowstorm.

The man looked over at Gene and asked him if he "wanted another brew." He was surprised when Gene, grinning widely, replied: "Sure, I'll have one with a fellow Kriegi from Stalag VII-A."

They failed to recognize each other; the man had been the camp medical doctor overseeing American casualties. Gene never had any interaction with him as it was his policy to avoid doctors at all costs. He explained to Gene he would routinely interact with the camp commandant, "SS" Colonel Hoffman, as Hoffman spoke fluent English and enjoyed the doctor's company.

A few days prior to Patton's arrival, Hoffman had shown him a communique from Berlin wherein Adolf Hitler was directing Hoffman to execute all the prisoners of war in the camp. Hoffman declared he had never disobeyed an order in his entire career but he would not follow that one. Gene realized how close he had come to death without even knowing it. The two former Stalag-mates had a couple of beers together that snowy evening. They never ran into each other again.

Gene met Sergeant Leonard A. Funk at a 508th Airborne reunion in El Paso, Texas, around 1980. Funk was conversing with a couple of people, but when he saw Gene he immediately ran to him and grabbed his hand, shaking it vigorously and wearing a huge smile. He explained to Gene he had always felt badly about pulling him from the hospital and had believed, during all the intervening years, Gene had been killed. He explained seeing Gene alive was like "lifting a heavy weight" from his back.

Gene with his old USC head coach, the legendary Rod "Bud" Dedeaux.

After they had a couple of drinks Gene realized Funk had mellowed out a great deal and was congenial and conversant. He was nothing like the exacting and overbearing sergeant he had been in 1944 when he made Gene and Meade "mow" so many meadows with their bayonets. Gene recalled he was more afraid of Funk than he was of the Germans. When Gene complained it was his fault he spent eight months as a POW Funk replied: "What the hell are you complaining about—you lived didn't you?" It proved to be the last time they saw each other and provided some closure for them both.

Gene would also run into Paul Pavlis, another friend he hadn't seen since they jumped. Paul was shocked and happy to see him alive. He explained to Gene he had inquired with Funk as to what happened to him back when they were still in Nijmegen. Funk wouldn't answer him and, in fact, quickly turned his back on him and walked away.

One day, while at home in Arizona, Gene answered his phone to find a German-accented voice on the other end. The man explained he

Gene and Medal of Honor recipient Sergeant Leonard A. Funk.

and a few of his friends were former guards at Stalag VII-A and were living in Sun City, Arizona. They heard through the grapevine Gene had been at the Stalag and were curious if he knew what had become of their commandant, "SS" Colonel Hoffman. They were sad to learn from Gene he had been killed.

These days Gene and his wife prefer to spend their summers in Colorado, rather than in the midst of the desert heat in Arizona. A few years ago, while in Buena Vista, Colorado, Gene received a phone call from someone who identified himself as "Elmer Melchi." Gene had no idea who Elmer Melchi might be and thought it was a crank call until Melchi began explaining he was the man Gene carried to the hospital tent in Stalag XII-A.

Melchi told him before the war he lived in Champaign, Illinois, a little under 200 miles south of DeKalb. When he finally made it home, one of the first things he did was travel to DeKalb to look Gene up and thank him. He managed to learn where he lived and met his parents, but Gene was absent. Gene's mom told Melchi he had gone to California and didn't really know how to reach him yet. Melchi gave her his contact information and asked her to let Gene know he had stopped in to thank him whenever Gene might phone her.

Gene's mom lost the note and some weeks passed before Gene made the expensive long-distance telephone call home. His mom mentioned "something about a paratrooper who came looking for you," but couldn't recall any details about the caller. She was getting up in age so her forgetfulness was unintentional. Gene never gave it another thought until Melchi phoned him decades later.

Melchi said he still had three of the four bullets in him and all the news media outlets wanted to cover their reunion. Gene was shocked. He was also very curious to meet the man for whom he had put his life at risk and whose blood he wore on his uniform for so long. They met the following day.

Melchi explained to Gene he had met a nurse at the Red Cross in Nottingham, England, had fallen head-over-heels in love, married her after the war, and brought his new wife to the United States. They lived in Colorado City, which is where Gene was staying when someone

Gene is on the left and Elmer Melchi is on the right.

mentioned they knew of another 82nd Airborne paratrooper in town. That led to Melchi contacting Gene. While Fox News covered the reunion locally, it was picked up and broadcast nationally by ABC, CBS, and NBC.

Gene continues to paint in watercolor, oils, and pencil sketches. He has placed his art in lodges and various commercial settings across the western United States and continues to sell his art. He and his wife live a very active lifestyle, appreciating each day as it arrives.

Gene Metcalfe says:

> America is everything you'd ever want in a country. Anything else is a distant second best and doesn't compare to what we have here in the U.S.

As for his World War II experiences, he says:

> I wouldn't give a dime for them, yet I wouldn't take a million bucks for them either.

A final note on Operation *Market Garden*:

Since August the Luftwaffe and the Wehrmacht had been on the defensive and retreating behind the frontier of Germany, so we were inclined to go about our planning with more preoccupation with our own plans than any concerns for the enemy, since his resistance was expected to be negligible.

General James Maurice "Jumpin, Jim" Gavin, March 22, 1907–February 23, 1990, in recollecting the Allied planning for Operation Market Garden.

Looking Back in Sketches

Over the course of the last few years I have spent countless hours engaging in a series of conversations with Gene Metcalfe. I refer to them as conversations rather than interviews for the reason they truly were exchanges of thoughts and experiences, not simply questions and answers.

Each time I think of our meetings, and of Gene, I smile. To know him is to love his perspective on life and to respect him as a truly extraordinary man wrapped in a somewhat ordinary-appearing wrapper.

Gene has impressed upon me the value of humor. He doesn't just give lip service to the concept of humor as a crucial part of life; he lives it. The following sketches reflect his persona better than I could do in a hundred thousand words. I trust you will enjoy them as much as I have.

Gene at home while being interviewed by Marcus A. Nannini in January 2018.

A medic noting the time is 1430 hours in Lent, Holland, September 18, 1944.

"Don't fire; it'll give us away!"

Himmler and interpreter.

Map with three circles.

Guard smoking a cigarette.

Women being presented with their "Lebensborn" medals.

Shaking down the prisoners returning from a day's labor in München.

Lone sentry with arms behind his back guarding a road in the middle of nowhere.

Gene and Dr. LaBorde in a München jail.

Billy making good on his promise.

Former Russian POW shaking down a German citizen on the road to München.

WAR CLAIMS COMMISSION
WASHINGTON 25, D. C.

July 13, 1953

Mr. Eugene C. Metcalfe
7601. Man   nue
Garde.   ....:.

WCC Claim Number___________

Dear Mr. Metcalfe:

Your claim for compensation for inhumane treatment and/or compulsory labor, pursuant to Public Law 303, 82nd Congress, April 9, 1952 (section 6 (d) of the War Claims Act of 1948, as amended), was adjudicated on __June 2.___, 1953 and an award in the sum of $____328.50____ has been made to you.

However, the Commission cannot certify your claim to the Treasury for payment at this time, since the money in the War Claims Fund for the payment of such claims was exhausted as of the close of business May 22, 1953. The War Claims Fund from which these claims are paid consists of the net proceeds of liquidated German and Japanese assets. When additional deposits are made into the War Claims Fund, your claim will be certified to the Treasury and a check in the amount stated above will be mailed to you by the Treasury Department.

Very truly yours,

War Claims Commission

Chairman

Vice Chairman

Commissioner

WCC Fm 195
7/1953

Gene's claim remains unpaid despite occasional follow-up inquiries.

Gene and his wife, Paulette, present day.